NO COMPROMISE!

By Arnold Whitridge

CRITICAL VENTURES IN MODERN FRENCH LITERATURE

DR. ARNOLD OF RUGBY

ALFRED DE VIGNY

MEN IN CRISIS: A STUDY OF THE REVOLUTIONS OF 1848

SIMON BOLIVAR

NO COMPROMISE!

The Story of the Fanatics

Who Paved the Way to the Civil War

BY ARNOLD WHITRIDGE

"Fanatics have their dreams, wherewith they weave
A paradise for a sect."

JOHN KEATS

GREENWOOD PRESS, PUBLISHERS
WESTPORT, CONNECTICUT

Library of Congress Cataloging in Publication Data

Whitridge, Arnold, 1891-
   No compromise!

    Reprint of the ed. published by Farrar, Straus
and Cudahy, New York.
    Bibliography: p.
    1. United States--History--Civil War, 1861-1865--
Causes. 2. United States--Politics and government--
1849-1861. I. Title.
[E415.7.W6 1974]   973.7'11   73-11626
ISBN 0-8371-7077-X

CONTENTS

Introduction   7

1. The Southern Fanatics   15

2. The Abolitionists   85

3. The Search for the Middle Way   149

    Bibliographical Notes   197

    Index   209

INTRODUCTION

THIS is a book about fanatics, about the handful of men North and South who fostered hatred between the two sections of the country, who magnified everything that might lead to misunderstanding, blocked every effort at compromise, and finally drove a reluctant people into a war they did not want to fight. As soon as Fort Sumter was fired on and the nation was committed to war, their work was done. Rhett and Yancey, the Southern fire-eaters who preached secession long before it became a respectable doctrine, were excluded from any share in the affairs of the Confederacy. Perhaps that is why the rising tide of Civil War books has swept around them, leaving them high and dry. Another ferocious fire-eater, Edmund Ruffin, the agricultural expert, fought in the Confederate ranks during the war, and finally died by his own hand in 1865 rather than live in a Yankee-dominated Virginia. John Brown, the greatest artist in antislavery propaganda of them all, died on the scaffold in 1859. Garrison, who did more than any one man to teach the North to hate slaveholders as well as slavery, was repudiated by the Republican party. Wendell Phillips, the incomparable orator—"an infernal machine set to music," as a Southern editor described him—played no part in the war except to abuse Lincoln for not emancipating the slaves sooner.

7

These fanatics and their disciples were not evil men nor, if you granted their hypotheses, were they unreasonable. Their sincerity as well as their ability was generally recognized, but they were nonetheless directly responsible for the breakdown of the democratic machinery by means of which the war might have been avoided. Thanks to them slavery was drowned in blood, but thanks to them also the real problem, the adjustment of the two races, remained unsolved. Fundamentally the abolitionists and the fire-eaters were alike. The extreme abolitionist interpreted the Constitution just as the extreme advocate of States' rights did. They both thought of it as the bulwark of slavery. The difference was that William Lloyd Garrison hated the Constitution and burned a copy of it on one occasion before a circle of admiring friends, whereas Barnwell Rhett revered it as the embodiment of all reason, something too sacrosanct to be discussed by Northern infidels.

"Would to God," wrote Garrison, "that the people of the North, without distinction of party, could see that the time has come for a separation from the South . . . in obedience to the 'Higher Law'! Is it not self-evident that we are and must be, with slave institutions in one section and free institutions in the other, two nations?" The Charleston *Mercury*, the organ of the Rhett family, never stated the case for secession more clearly. As soon as the fighting began, Garrison conveniently forgot what he had said about two nations, and shouted "Thank God for the war" as loudly as anybody.

The Southern extremist was equally delighted. Before the outbreak of war he had had an uneasy feeling that a good many of his friends, even though they called themselves secessionists, were still looking back over their shoulders. They hoped that an "arrangement" might yet be possible. As a

8

member of the Alabama legislature warned Jefferson Davis
when the Confederate government was deliberating whether
to fire on Fort Sumter: "Unless you sprinkle blood in the
face of the Southern people they will be back in the Union
in less than ten days." The difficulty of getting the South out
of the Union has sometimes been underestimated. John Chesnut, a widely respected South Carolina slaveholder, expressed
a view that must have been shared by many others: "Without
the aid and countenance of the whole United States we could
not have kept slavery. I always knew the world was against
us. That was the only reason I was a Union man. I wanted all
the power the United States gave me, to hold my own."

The "irrepressible conflict," which William H. Seward
predicted in a speech in Rochester in 1858, was not yet at that
time by any means irrepressible. Seward himself, fearing he
had gone too far, tried to "clarify" his remarks afterward, but
the fanatics on both sides of the border made sure that those
words should never be forgotten. John Brown's raid in the
following year was a godsend to them. In the South the fire-
eaters insisted the raid proved that the Republicans were spon-
soring a Negro insurrection, in which case the conflict really
would be irrepressible. At the same time many Northerners
interpreted the ill-fated phrase as meaning that Seward had
wind of a wide-spread Southern conspiracy to break up the
Union. No such conspiracy ever existed except in the minds
of Rhett, Yancey, Ruffin and a few of their followers. Every
time they tried to influence State legislatures in the direction
of secession they were snubbed. At no time was there any
concerted plan in the South leading to secession. There was
as much variety of opinion on the questions at issue in the
South as in the North. Unfortunately radical Republicans, on

the fringes of the Abolitionist party if not abolitionists themselves, believed in the Southern conspiracy, just as Southerners
came to believe that Northern manufacturers and capitalists
had joined forces with the abolitionists to overthrow the constitutional rights of the slave States, tax the South for the
benefit of the North, and reduce the white man to the level
of the Negro.

If these myths could have been dispelled, there would have
been no war. Up to the very end Douglas was convinced that
the masses in the South were not in sympathy with secession,
and as one who toured extensively in the South during the
campaign of 1860 he was in a position to know. The popular
vote in that election seems to have justified his opinion. Georgia and Louisiana as well as the States of the upper South
went for Bell, the candidate of the Constitutional Union party,
or for Douglas himself, the standard bearer of the conservative
Democrats, indicating that the people in those States had no
desire to follow the lead of the fire-eaters. No historian has
yet accounted for the failure of this great weight of public
opinion to make itself felt during the critical period between
Lincoln's election and the firing on Sumter. At no time in
their history have the American people seemed so incapable
of controlling their destiny.

Why did the Southern voters who were opposed to secession in November, 1860, even after Lincoln's election, change
their opinions during the next three months and decide there
was no future for them within the Union? Why did Lincoln
make no effort to counteract the propaganda depicting him
as an enemy of the South? Why did he make no public statement of his policies at any time between his election and his
inauguration? Why did the movement in favor of the Crit-

tenden Compromise collapse in spite of the fact that mammoth petitions were submitted to Congress urging its support? Why was the Washington Peace Conference not called before, instead of after, the lower South had seceded? Possibly the activities of Rhett and Yancey, of Garrison, Phillips, John Brown and Sumner, may provide a clue to the answer of some of these questions, and even to the much greater question of why the war had to be fought at all.

That there were real grievances and anxieties in both sections of the country was obvious. These men did not create the grievances, but by their incessant propaganda they so upset the emotional balance North and South that any suggestion of conciliation, any appeal to common sense, was made to appear like treason or cowardice in disguise. The fanatic, the man for whom John Randolph says there is no stopping point in life, has never been a popular figure, but in the greatest crisis in American history it was the fanatic who called the tune. Never has the cry "no compromise" been raised with more terrible results.

ONE

The Southern Fanatics

I

Noʀᴛʜ of the Mason-Dixon line, John Caldwell Calhoun
has always been regarded as the villain of the piece, the master
architect of the treasonable doctrine of secession. We read of
debates with Daniel Webster on the nature of the Constitution, debates in which Webster is shown as emerging glori-
ously triumphant; but everything else to do with Calhoun, his
defense of the minority against the weight of numbers, his
insistence that the power of government must somehow be
controlled, is conveniently forgotten. Walt Whitman tells of
a conversation he overheard between two wounded soldiers,
in which one of them maintained that the real monument
to Calhoun was not the marble shaft in Charleston erected to
his memory by friends and admirers, but "the ruined South,
the generation of young men destroyed, society torn up by the
roots, and the name of Southerner blackened with shame."

Time has softened this verdict, but the picture of a misspent
life devoted to undermining the republic still lingers in the
back of our minds. Calhoun's own contemporaries, even those
who disagreed with him, would have been amazed at any such
estimate. To them the political philosophy of the austere
Carolinian was anything but absurd. On the day of his death
Henry Clay and Daniel Webster bore witness on the floor of

the Senate to his "transcendent talents" and to the purity of his "exalted patriotism." Webster could think of no man "more assiduous in the discharge of his appropriate duties," no man who "wasted less of life in what is called recreation." Perhaps that was just the trouble. Calhoun was never recreated by the changing world in which he lived. He was a fervent nationalist when he first entered public life, and at the same time a devout believer in the Constitution as a safeguard against oppression by section or class. Such he remained until his death in 1850.

In the early days of the Republic there was nothing peculiar to the South in the doctrine of States' rights. It was as dear to New England as it was to Virginia. If the Virginia and Kentucky Resolutions developed the idea that the Constitution was a "compact" between sovereign States, the language of the Hartford Convention was no less explicit. The New Englanders who met together at Hartford in 1814 to protest against "Mr. Madison's war" asserted the right and duty of a State to interpose its authority for the protection of its citizens from infractions of the Constitution by the federal government. To portray Calhoun as the founder of an evil doctrine is a travesty of the facts. The doctrine was not evil, and Calhoun did not found it. He was racked, as only a genuine patriot could be, by the long conflict between his love for the Union and his love for the South, and by the ever increasing difficulty of defending a minority against the weight of numbers. In his own way he was as eager to preserve the Union as Daniel Webster himself. The tragedy was that what Calhoun wanted to preserve was a ghost, the ghost of America as he had first known it in the days of the Virginia dynasty.

"The cast-iron man," as Harriet Martineau described him,

seemed to her one of the tragic figures of all time. This practical, hard-headed Englishwoman, one of the best reporters of
the Washington scene in the eighteen-thirties, would never
forget "the splendid eye, the straight forehead, surmounted
by a load of stiff, upright, dark hair; the stern brow; the
inflexible mouth. . . ." "One of the most remarkable heads in
the country," thought Miss Martineau (it was an age that
studied phrenology) and yet there was something inhuman
too about Mr. Calhoun. "He would come in sometimes to
keep our understandings upon a painful stretch for a short
while, and leave us to take to pieces his close, rapid, theoreti-
cal talk, and see what we could make of it. We found it
usually more worth retaining as a curiosity than as either very
just or useful . . . his theories of government, (almost the only
subject on which his thoughts are employed,) the squarest
and compactest theories that ever were made, are composed of
limited elements, and are not therefore likely to stand service
very well." How different he was from Mr. Webster, "lean-
ing back at his ease, telling stories, cracking jokes, shaking
the sofa with burst after burst of laughter," or from the
homely Mr. Clay, "sitting upright on the sofa, with his snuff-
box ever in his hand," who discoursed so charmingly in soft
even tones on any of the great subjects of American policy.

No historian has ever improved on Miss Martineau's pro-
files of these statesmen. Had she only visited Washington a
few years earlier, while John Randolph was still alive, she
might have given us an equally telling portrait of that erratic
but strangely gifted character who, more than anyone else,
was responsible for the cast-iron quality of Calhoun's ideas.
John Randolph of Roanoke was the man who led Calhoun
step by step to identify slavery with States' rights. A Virginia

aristocrat, direct descendant of John Rolfe and Pocahontas, Randolph prided himself on his love of liberty and his hatred of equality. He waged a savage war against anything and everything that threatened the planter economy under which he had grown up. Internal improvements, the tariff, the Bank, foreign wars, they were all anathema to him in that they benefited one State at the expense of another. "Asking one of the States to surrender part of her sovereignty was like asking a lady to surrender part of her chastity." For him, every man in Congress was a delegate of his State, not of the people of the United States at large. "How shall a man from Mackinaw or the Yellowstone River respond to the sentiments of the people who live in New Hampshire? It is as great a mockery, —a greater mockery than to talk to these colonies about their virtual representation in the British Parliament."

John Randolph felt himself a citizen of Virginia rather than of the United States, and he flaunted that belief in Congress with remarkable consistency for over thirty years. Before we dismiss him as the champion of a hopelessly lost cause, we might well remember that he was the first man in America to protest against "the strange notion which lately has seized the minds of men that all things must be done for them by the Government, and that they can do nothing for themselves. The Government is not only to attend to the great concerns which are its province, but it must step in and ease individuals of their natural and real obligations."

Randolph was not a democrat, not a nationalist, and not a liberal, nor did he share the popular American belief that change necessarily meant reform, and that expansion must bring progress in its wake. On the contrary, he followed Burke in believing that a disposition to preserve was just as much a characteristic of good government as the determination to change. Expansion he resented as heralding the downfall of the authority of the original thirteen States. "No Government, extending from the Atlantic to the Pacific, can be fit to govern me or those whom I represent." So he proclaimed in 1822, and in the same year he pointed out the danger to the Union in the steady increase of Western States. The way of life he envisaged would never survive in a vast nation stretching across the continent.

Randolph's ideal society did not differ much from that of his kinsman, Thomas Jefferson. Until he became President, Jefferson too believed in a strictly agricultural America, a nation of independent farmers trading with the "workshops of Europe," with perhaps a sprinkling of better-educated planters to furnish suitable leadership. When Jefferson reluctantly came to recommend the encouragement of American factories, Randolph parted company with him. He maintained that "America was as unsuited for really profitable manufacturing as England was for really profitable agriculture." Holding the beliefs that he did about the supreme importance of agriculture and the sanctity of States' rights, it was inevitable that Randolph should have felt compelled to defend the institution of slavery. The task did not come easily to him. As a young man he had heard denunciations of slavery by fellow Virginians such as George Mason, Jefferson, and his own stepfather, St. John Tucker, for whom he had the greatest respect. He referred to himself half jokingly as "*l'ami des noirs*," and there was more than a little truth in his claim. No slaveholder was more beloved than John Randolph. He never bought or sold a Negro, and he never wavered in his denunciation of the slave trade. At the end of his life he confirmed his grant of freedom and land to his "poor slaves." Even Whittier, the poet laureate of the Abolitionists, acknowledged that Randolph was a humane master.

And yet, though Randolph never spoke of slavery as a positive good, as Calhoun did, he was just as adamant as Calhoun in denouncing the folly of government interference with slavery. Henry Adams has excoriated the "deliberate, cold-blooded attempt to pervert the old and honorable principle of States' rights into a mere tool for the protection of Negro slavery, which Randolph professed to think the worst of all earthly misfortunes." It is unfortunately true that John Randolph, the "purist in politics," was not above appealing to Southern prejudices for the defense of the society he loved. "He might himself oppose slavery but he would not refuse the support of those who inclined towards the institution." He probably would have excused himself on the plea that though slavery was an evil, a cancer on the body politic, the remedies proposed would be worse than the disease. Governmental interference between the master and the slave might well lead to a black insurrection or to a repetition of the recent and continuing horrors in Haiti.

At the end of his life when he was going insane, and when he thought the Abolitionists were putting a torch to his property, he came near to advocating what he really abhorred. At other times he had no hesitation in saying that slavery was a curse to the master. On one occasion he told Josiah Quincy that the greatest orator he had ever heard was a woman. "She was a slave. She was a mother, and her rostrum was the auction block." No doubt Randolph believed, as many other Southerners did though they were ashamed to say so, that ultimately economic changes would make slavery unprofitable, and that it would disappear just as serfdom had disappeared in England. The fact that in 1860 it was dying out in the Border States, and that in spite of all the efforts of Southern fanatics it would not take root in the Territories, suggests that Randolph may well have been right, but by that time the national capacity for patience was exhausted. Pending the death of slavery from natural causes, Randolph was determined to wall it off from external interference. It was not a subject that lay within the jurisdiction of the federal government.

John Calhoun was far more of a nationalist than John Randolph; indeed at first glance the two men seemed to have nothing in common. The sober Calvinist Calhoun, who never allowed himself a moment's relaxation, and the scoffing aristocratic Randolph, arrived at their common destination by different routes. They learned to respect each other, and Randolph finally sensed the fact that Calhoun was his greatest disciple, but they never became friends. It was natural enough in the excitement of 1812 for Calhoun, a War Hawk like most of the people from the back country who thought the British were stirring up Indian uprisings, to ride roughshod over what must have seemed to him the pusillanimous objections of the irascible gentleman from Roanoke. A few years later when Calhoun came forward with a strangely modern sounding appeal, "Let us conquer space" (meaning let us bind the country together with roads and canals), he was irritated again by Randolph's nagging objections. It was not until 1824, when South Carolina was beginning to feel the pinch of the tariff, that he remembered Randolph's forebodings. However patriotic the motive may be, Randolph had warned him, the direct taxes, the large navy, the well-drilled army, the roads and canals and subsidized industry all tended to consolidate and strengthen the national government at the expense of the States.

The tariff opened Calhoun's eyes to the danger of arraying the great geographic interests of the Union against one another. From then on, without losing his affection for the Union, he turned more and more toward a strict construction of the Constitution, and to a belief in the overriding importance of States' rights. As the excitement over the tariff died down, the agitation over slavery took its place. Even so Calhoun always flinched from the final step of secession. To the end of his life his fertile brain was conjuring up one scheme after another by means of which the two sections of the country might yet live together in harmony.

Calhoun's religious, political and economic beliefs were all closely intertwined. Brought up as a Calvinist, he accepted without question the doctrine that God had predestined a chosen few to eternal life, whereas the rest of mankind had been condemned to eternal darkness. The subsequent identification of the chosen few with slaveholders, and the rest of mankind with slaves, may seem to us a preposterous corollary, but there was nothing preposterous about it to Calhoun. He examined the institution of slavery and rationalized his beliefs about it with complete honesty. His religion taught him that the chief end of man was to know and do the will of God. Obviously it was the will of God, since it was an inescapable law of society, that one portion of society depended upon the labors of the other. In the Southern States where two dissimilar races lived side by side, the relationship of master and slave was the only relationship that would enable the two races to live together in peace. As obstinate as the abolitionists,

22

whom in many ways he resembled, Calhoun was as incapable as they were of finding a middle way.

II

The real architect of secession was neither John Randolph nor John Calhoun. They laid the foundations, but it was Robert Barnwell Rhett, a second-rate South Carolina politician, who reared the building and finally, after much persuasion, induced the South to occupy it. Rhett never commanded the respect or the affection of his State. He was not at home with the classics, as Randolph was, and he did not possess Calhoun's qualities of patience and self-control, but he was more ready than either of them to abide by the consequences of his words. Unlike them he contemplated the break-up of the Union without fear and without regret. Even if South Carolina had to take the plunge alone, he was willing to gamble on the other States joining her. Except for a short time in 1860, just after South Carolina had voted herself out of the Union, Rhett was never a popular figure in the South, but he successfully exploited one weapon to which his opponents could find no answer—the terrible certainty of the fanatic. While they counseled delay, compromise, further discussion, he demanded immediate action. For thirty years he kept on reminding them that his was the only way.

As soon as he stopped ranting about secession and Southern independence this *enfant terrible* of South Carolina politics became a model citizen. A lawyer and a devout churchman, vice-president of the Young Men's Temperance Society, secretary of the Charleston Port Association for promoting the

Christian gospel among seamen, and a prominent member of the South Carolina Society for the Advancement of Learning, he represented all that was most respectable in Charleston society. He married twice, both times very happily, and produced a large family of devoted children. Though they suffered great hardships as a result of his policies, no member of the family ever doubted the wisdom of his decisions. To his oldest son, who as editor of the Charleston *Mercury* became the spokesman of his views, he was a man without flaw. Outside of the family circle he was generally considered a dangerous extremist, but no one ever questioned his courage or his honesty. Even a staunch Unionist like James L. Petigru, who hated everything Rhett stood for, was ready and eager to lend him money when he was in difficulties.

Robert Barnwell Smith—the name was changed to Rhett in 1837—was born at Beaufort, in the southernmost corner of South Carolina, on December 21, 1800. On both sides his family had played a distinguished part in the history of the State. Rhett was proud to be descended from Sir John Yeamans, the founder of Charleston and one of the first governors of the colony. Another ancestor had won renown in colonial days by his exploits against pirates. His father had fought against the British at the siege of Savannah, though he was only a boy at the time, and again at Charleston, where he was made prisoner.

By a strange quirk of fate he was distantly related on his mother's side to John Quincy Adams, but it was not a relationship either of them cared to claim. Adams mentions Rhett several times in his famous *Diary*, and always with the greatest contempt. He describes him as "a compound of wild democracy and iron-bound slavery, combined with the feudal

cramp of state sovereignty—the mongrel blood of nullification." Everything about him was objectionable. He howled
his speeches, "his head thrown back as he spoke, with his face
upwards, like that of a howling dog." The kind blue eyes,
the ready smile, the instinctive courtesy, all the characteristics
which were so obvious to his children, escaped Mr. Adams'
notice.

After a few years' schooling at Beaufort, Rhett moved to
North Carolina. His father had bought a plantation on the
Cape Fear River, but the venture proved a failure and Rhett
was soon back in Charleston studying law. He was elected
to the State legislature in 1826 and shortly afterward he became involved in the great controversy over nullification.
It was the passage by Congress of the tariff of 1828, the
so-called "tariff of abominations," that launched him upon
his career as a crusader and revolutionist. Rhett, who had
started out as a flamboyant nationalist, quickly came to the
conclusion that in one way or another, either through regula-
tions of the federal government or through the legerdemain
of trade, the South was being made to contribute to the prosperity of the North without getting an adequate return. From
that moment he became a fanatical States' rights man. The
"abominations" were removed from the tariff in 1832, but by
that time it was too late. The chimera of nullification had
already been engendered.

The doctrine of nullification was based on the premise that
the Constitution was a compact between sovereign States.
Any other conception, the idea for instance that the Constitution was established by and for the people living in the
thirteen colonies, that it was the collective act of the whole
American people, Calhoun considered dangerous and hereti-

cal. It followed from this doctrine that the States as sovereigns had the right to judge when their agent, the federal government, had exceeded its powers. It was always possible for a State to call a convention of its own people, pronounce an objectionable law null and void, and prevent its execution within its own limits. The scheme was represented as an admirable remedy, safe, speedy, effective and, above all, peaceful. Nullification did not contemplate revolution or civil war. It was within the Constitution, not opposed to it.

By this line of reasoning Calhoun may have satisfied himself that his position was logically impregnable, but he did not convince anybody outside of South Carolina, not even John Randolph who thought nullification was nonsense though he denied the right of the federal government to coerce a sovereign State—and, least of all, Andrew Jackson. Even in South Carolina the Charleston *Courier*, a conservative paper as compared to the *Mercury*, denounced nullification as a strange doctrine "which upholds the Constitution by violating it, preserves peace by declaring war, and perpetuates the Union by formally declaring for its dissolution." Jackson threatened to throw an army into South Carolina at the first sign of resistance to the revenue officers, but a compromise, urged by Clay and accepted by Calhoun, restored the peace. The nullification ordinance was repealed, the planters went back to their cotton fields, nullifiers and Union men found themselves running for the legislature on the same ticket, and the danger of revolution was forgotten—for the time being.

Throughout all this agitation Rhett was like a man possessed. Where Calhoun walked warily, making sure that his followers were close behind him, Rhett marched boldly ahead without looking to left or right, equally indifferent to opposition or support. If, as Jefferson had said, the tree of liberty must now and again be watered with the blood of patriots, so be it! Rhett harked back to the Revolution, insisting that the issues involved between South Carolina and the federal government were essentially the same as those that had separated the colonies from the British crown. What was the difference between George III's tea tax and the protective tariff the government was trying to impose on South Carolina? "George Washington was a disunionist," said Rhett, "Samuel Adams, Patrick Henry, Jefferson and Rutledge were all disunionists and traitors . . . and for maintaining the very constitutional principles for which we now contend. . . . If a Confederacy of the Southern States could now be obtained, should we not deem it a happy termination—happy beyond expectation, of our long struggle for our rights against oppression?"

This was strong meat even for South Carolina. An old veteran of the Revolution who had hobbled into the Convention hall on his crutches to hear the speeches was so shocked by this veiled attack on the government that he interrupted the proceedings to proclaim his love for the Union and his readiness to fight for it again. Rhett saw at once that he had gone too far. Except for his own constituents from Beaufort, whom he had already converted, no one in the audience was ready for another revolution. Reluctantly he fell into line behind Calhoun and explained that he too prided himself on his devotion to the Union, but to the Union as it was originally conceived.

After recovering from his nullification wounds, Rhett entered into what was for him a conservative phase. As a loyal supporter of Calhoun, he convinced himself that the Constitution rightly interpreted could still be used as an effective safeguard of Southern interests. The tariff, after all, was only one of the symptoms of the general disease of consolidation, a disease which might well be cured if the former nullifiers could get control of the Democratic party. Rhett's friends in the meantime had been urging him to run for Congress, where his talents might show to better advantage than in his own State. Not much persuasion was needed. His appetite for office had been whetted but not satisfied by his experience in local politics. In the years following the nullification debate, he had had time to supplement a sketchy education by extensive reading in history and political economy. If he was still arrogant, as his opponents charged, he was also better informed. There was always too much of the conscious aristocrat about him to please the general public, and for this reason the South never followed him as it did Calhoun, but his honesty, his courage and his ability were never questioned.

Rhett was elected to Congress in 1837 and soon made a name for himself as a loyal Van Buren supporter. As John Quincy Adams noted, "Mr. Rhett of South Carolina was passing from the chrysalis state of a late voracious nullifier to a painted administration butterfly." His support of Van Buren was not entirely disinterested. Rhett had now become Calhoun's campaign manager and, if Calhoun stepped into Van Buren's shoes, as he hoped to do, there was every chance that he in turn would take Calhoun's place in the Senate. The scheme seemed reasonable enough, but Calhoun was never quite able to grasp the coveted prize, which meant that Rhett did not reach the Senate until after Calhoun's death. By that time his hope of preserving the Union, never very strong in spite of Calhoun's insistence, had entirely evaporated.

The real issue now was not the tariff, which was a question for economists, or even States' rights, a subject which lent itself to friendly discussion among political philosophers, but slavery. Here was a great solid fact, "a positive good," according to Calhoun and Rhett, but to many of their fellow Southerners an affliction to be endured, but not discussed, until in God's good time it outlived its usefulness and disappeared. The founding fathers had always been troubled by slavery. It nagged at their conscience. Washington regretted it, Jefferson denounced it, while Hamilton and Franklin went still further by joining the abolition movement. Hamilton became secretary of the New York Abolition Society, and was requested by Lafayette to propose him as a fellow member. In the early days of the republic, there was no yawning gulf between the North and the South on the subject of slavery, and as late as 1826, of the 143 emancipation societies in the United States 103 were located in the South.

Unfortunately the world market for cotton and the acquisition of new lands to grow it on, thanks to the Louisiana Purchase, coupled with Eli Whitney's all too successful invention of the cotton gin, combined to make the South change its mind. Anything that contributed so tremendously to prosperity could hardly be regarded as an evil. Instead of being ashamed of slavery, the average Southerner began to look upon it as a great religious, social and moral blessing. The changing point of view in the South can be clearly traced in the language of its favorite statesman. As a young man, Calhoun conceded that slavery was an unnatural state, "a dark cloud that obscures half the lustre of our free institutions," but that was before slavery had forced its way into politics. As he grew older he veered from apology to active support.

"Many in the South," he admitted, "once believed that it was a moral and political evil; that folly and delusion are gone; we see it now in its true light, and regard it as the most safe and stable basis for free institutions in the world." This was a significant departure from Randolph who, though he denied the right of Congress to interfere with slavery, deprecated it politically and morally as an evil.

Calhoun would never have sprung to its defense if it had not been for the abolitionist petitions with which Congress was being flooded just at the time when the excitement over nullification was dying down. These petitions were at first directed at the slave trade in the District of Columbia, an evil which many slaveholders, including John Randolph, had also deplored. The debates in Congress in 1836 and 1837 over the reception of these petitions inflamed the zeal of the abolitionists. Though they were steadily making converts, and though their presses were multiplying, sober opinion in the North as well as the South condemned the abolitionists as irresponsible agitators. With the murder of Elijah Lovejoy, an abolitionist editor in Alton, Illinois, who was killed by a mob on November 7, 1837, while trying to defend his press, public opinion about abolitionism began to change. The reaction to his death throughout the North indicated that the anti-slavery movement could no longer be ignored.

Once again the blood of the martyrs proved the seed of the church. From being a few disorganized fanatics the abolitionists were gradually developing into a disciplined political body. Their propaganda provoked Southerners to an active defense of the institution their forefathers had deplored. Only five years earlier, in January 1832, an emancipation plan had been introduced into the Virginia legislature. After vigorous debate it passed the assembly, and only failed in the upper chamber by a single vote. Again and again during the next twenty years the forces of reason very nearly asserted themselves, but each time the fanatics just managed to sweep them aside.

During most of the year 1837, when Rhett was serving his first term in Congress, a financial panic distracted attention from the slavery question, but with the Lovejoy murder still occupying space in the press the slavery theme was back in prominence again by December. The demand of the republic of Texas to be admitted into the Union enabled free-soilers to conjure up a picture of black-hearted slave owners seeking "bigger pens to cram with slaves." Slavery was thus under fire politically as well as morally when William Slade, a quick-witted Congressman of Vermont, presented resolutions of the Vermont legislature favoring the suppression of slavery and the slave trade in the District of Columbia. The gag rule stating that all petitions on the subject of slavery "shall, without either being printed or referred, be laid upon the table, and that no further action shall be had thereon," had not yet been presented for that session so that Slade could not be prevented from speaking. His speech precipitated one of the angriest debates that had ever occurred in Congress, a debate so bitter that after adjournment the Southern members held a caucus to consider the dissolution of the Union.

Once again Rhett threatened revolution. He did not indulge in the offensive personalities that were to mark the speeches of men like Senator Wigfall of Texas, or Charles Sumner of Massachusetts, but he made it perfectly clear that the Constitution should be amended to suit the South, or else that the Union should be dissolved. Not that he expected either of these alternatives to be accepted, but he was determined to stake out a position which he knew the South would eventually have to occupy. While the ever cautious Calhoun was content with offering a series of resolutions in the Senate defining the nature of the Constitution and denouncing all attacks on slavery, Rhett, weary of what seemed to him the timidity of his Southern colleagues, had hurried back to South Carolina to whip up feeling in favor of his ultimatum to the government. Fearlessly he leaped ahead to the conclusion toward which Calhoun's own logic pointed. The very quickness of his ruthless intelligence betrayed him. Like many other inexperienced politicians, he was so convinced by his own reasoning that he lost touch with the very people he was trying to lead.

In all the unsuccessful attempts of the Southern bloc in Congress to adopt a concerted plan of action, Rhett made it clear that though he gladly acknowledged Calhoun's leadership he was not prepared to follow him blindfold. He reserved the right to conduct forays on his own account, even when the great man disapproved. On one occasion when, harking back to the days of nullification, he led another movement for separate State action on the tariff, Calhoun disapproved very definitely and had to summon all his resources to bring Rhett and his fellow radicals back into line. Calhoun always insisted that the Southern States should act as a unit and use the immense power that unity would give them to maintain equilibrium between the two sections of the nation.

Rhett, perhaps more realistic than Calhoun in spite of his impetuosity, knew that when it came to taking a stand against the national government the Southern States would never act as a unit, any more than the thirteen colonies had acted as a unit before the outbreak of the Revolution. In 1776 the ma-

jority of the colonists were not in favor of separation from
Great Britain, but thanks to men like Samuel Adams and
Patrick Henry, who poured oil on the fires of insurrection
whenever they threatened to subside, the Revolution was
achieved. In the same way Southern independence might
become a fact instead of a dream, provided one State could
be induced to take the lead.

At the end of the Van Buren administration Calhoun had
hoped to form a political alliance between the West and the
South on which he might ride to the Presidency, but Rhett
was not impressed by Calhoun's plans and felt that the South
must learn to fend for itself. Calhoun was not so easily discouraged. At the Memphis convention of 1845, called to promote western trade and internal improvements, he urged the
right of the federal government to increase the safety and
facility of commerce on the Mississippi River. With the help
of various other concessions to the Western States he hoped
to break up the alliance between the Northeast and the West.
Calhoun counted on the Mississippi steamboats to draw the
West into the Southern orbit but, as Arnold Toynbee has
pointed out, the locomotive has proved a more potent factor
in determining the course of American history than the
steamboat. The lines of communication within the Continent
switched from the vertical to the horizontal and, in spite of
Calhoun's efforts, the Northwest was detached from the South
and welded by interest as well as sentiment on to the Northeast.

The fact was that the Northwest, peopled largely by New
England stock and by German and Scandinavian immigrants,
was never sympathetic to slavery. Calhoun must have known
this as well as Rhett, but his fertile brain kept on searching

for new ways of safeguarding the South's position within the Union long after Rhett had given up the fight.

III

Rhett's eagerness to be rid of the Union met with another disappointment in the Senate's rejection of the Wilmot Proviso. Had this unprovoked assault upon Southern institutions, as Calhoun called it, been approved by the Senate, the South would have been tempted to secede at once. David Wilmot was a Pennsylvania Democrat who, like many other Northern Democrats, had been accused of being a tool of the slavery interests. In order to prove that a Northern Democrat could be independent, Wilmot proposed that slavery should be excluded from any Territories that might be acquired from Mexico as a result of the war. This move embarrassed President Polk, as well as Calhoun, neither of whom wanted the question of slavery raised. Polk was on the verge of completing his expansion program. The Oregon treaty had been signed and ratified and on August 8, 1846, he asked Congress for two million dollars with which he meant to bribe Mexico into ceding the vast area of California.

The Wilmot Proviso virtually told Polk he could have his two million dollars on the condition that any territory he acquired from the republic of Mexico should be forever free soil. The President was disgusted that an unknown young Congressman with no experience in national politics should take it upon himself to upset the delicate balance which wiser men than he had been at such pains to establish. As a practical politician eager to go down in history as the man who had fulfilled America's manifest destiny by winning Texas, Oregon and California, he did not want to be bothered about slavery. Calhoun was equally annoyed. Even if he did not want to extend the dominion of slavery at that particular moment, the attempt to prohibit it in the Territories involved a tacit condemnation of his cherished institution, which he considered highly offensive.

Rhett, on the other hand, was delighted. He would have welcomed anything that brought matters to a head. "I am sorry," he wrote to Calhoun, "to come to the conviction that there is no chance for the Wilmot Proviso or the abolition of slavery in the District of Columbia at the approaching Congress. Would to God they would do both, and let us have the contest, and end it once and forever. But the Northern statement will commit, I am satisfied, no such blunder."

Rhett's guess proved right. The Wilmot Proviso was narrowly defeated in the Senate but, though it did not become law, it served notice on the Southern States that they were in for a fight against containment. Slavery was to be bottled up and then extinguished. As the number of free States increased, the power and the prestige of the South would inevitably decline. Under these circumstances it was not unnatural that Southerners should have begun to talk about equality in the Union or independence out of it. More and more as the controversy developed, Southern orators anchored their case on the Constitution, while Northerners founded theirs on the Union. As Senator Toombs of Georgia put it, "the cry of Union is the masked battery from behind which the Constitution and the rights of the South are to be assailed."

The furor over the Wilmot Proviso completed Rhett's conversion to disunion. He had served the Polk administration faithfully as an ardent expansionist, and he was now determined to devote himself entirely to the interests of his own State. Calhoun was failing rapidly, and Rhett looked forward to taking his place in the Senate as the spokesman of the South. While he did not yet call himself a secessionist, he was already advocating a temporary dissolution of the Union as the only means of preserving the Constitution. Such wild talk did not endear him to the prosperous and generally conservative planters of South Carolina. The big slaveholders in the South were mostly Whigs who, for the sake of party unity as well as for safety, wanted to play down all the agitation over the abolitionists. They also opposed aggressive tactics for the extension of slavery. In this circle Rhett was considered too excitable, too lacking in tact or discretion, ever to wear the mantle of Calhoun.

The Great Compromise of 1850 was everywhere hailed with delight, except by a few fanatics in the North as well as in the South who felt that politicians were merely papering over cracks in the walls instead of strengthening foundations. Southerners in general, sick of the Congressional wrangling over slavery and longing above all things to be let alone, were more than willing to entrust their case to Henry Clay. The gist of Clay's compromise package was the immediate admission of California as a free State, the organization of Territorial governments in New Mexico and Utah without mention of slavery, a strong Fugitive Slave Law, and the abolition of the domestic slave trade in the District of Columbia.

On February 5, Clay, a sick man at the time, began his great speech in support of these resolutions. The Senate chamber had been specially heated for the occasion, and the janitor had done his work so well that the thermometer stood at one hundred degrees. Ladies in hooped skirts and perspiring gentlemen crowded the Senate floor and overflowed into the corridors. Clay spoke for three hours and then, exhausted, gave way to an adjournment. He finished his remarks on the following day. It was a speech glowing with love for the Union. Clay had a way of charming his audience that neither of his great rivals could equal. Calhoun might be more relentlessly logical, Webster better informed and more impressive physically, but it was Henry Clay who won his way into men's hearts.

For the next month nothing was talked of in Washington but Clay's magnificent plea for compromise. Though he had swept his audience off their feet, Congress and the nation as a whole were not yet converted. The issue was still trembling in the balance when Webster made his great speech of conciliation in support of Clay's resolutions. He spoke as a nationalist, as an American, and above all as a man who felt himself in tune with the age. Webster saw that slavery was doomed. Eli Whitney's cotton gin had given it a few more years of life, but time was against it. He was willing, therefore, in spite of his belief that slavery was a moral and political evil, to give it full constitutional rights. The Union was worth temporary concessions. Whatever might befall him in the North, he would devote himself to the advocacy of Clay's plan.

The speech made a tremendous sensation. New England radicals were aghast. Whittier mourned for the fallen statesman whose faith was lost and whose honor was dead. Webster was a "Benedict Arnold," a man who had struck a terrible blow at freedom. Southerners, on the other hand, saw in Webster's speech a guarantee that Clay's compromises would be passed. They began to hesitate. Calhoun's death in the end of March hastened the disintegration of the Southern forces. Soon the whole country was rallying to the Compromise. Calhoun's gloomy predictions were forgotten, and Webster and Clay were acclaimed as heroes. The New Orleans *Daily Delta* called Webster's speech a godsend—"like the trident of Old Neptune, calming the excited sea and soothing the raging billows."

The success of Clay's Compromise seemed to have struck a death blow at Southern disunionism. In his final speech Clay, referring specifically to Rhett and William Lowndes Yancey, already known as the two most truculent advocates of States' rights, spoke of them as "men who live by agitation. It is their meat, their bread, the air which they breathe." Then, turning to Rhett's cousin Senator Barnwell who had risen to expostulate, he added that if Rhett had pronounced the sentiments attributed to him, and that if he were to follow up those sentiments by corresponding overt acts, "he will be a traitor, and I hope he will meet the fate of a traitor." The galleries broke into a tumult of applause. (Allan Nevins, *Ordeal of the Union*, I, 339.)

The Charleston *Mercury* hailed Rhett as the Patrick Henry of the day. "Oh! that we were all such traitors." But the South Carolina planters were not yet ready to be stampeded by the *Mercury*. They settled back with a sigh of relief, more interested in the price of cotton than in the reckless politics of the Rhett family.

Clay's apparently successful effort to settle the slavery controversy once and for all marked the low point in Rhett's career. Rhett had been elected to the Senate in 1850, but as soon as he saw the tide was running against secession he resigned his seat. His resignation was hailed by his Unionist friends as the brightest feather in his cap. Here was a man who had tried to break up the Union, and the people had decided against him. Let them select someone to take his place, thought Rhett, who was more ready to submit to Northern dictation. Once again he would bide his time until the slow-moving South had caught up with him.

IV

Another fire-eater, William Lowndes Yancey, who protested against the Compromise no less vigorously than Rhett, was equally unsuccessful in overcoming the lazy optimism of the average Southern voter. All over the South the foes of the Compromise were routed, and sectionalism rebuked. The people of Alabama, Yancey's own State, would listen to him by the hour and they would applaud his shrewd hits at the Yankee hucksters, but they would not vote for him. Wherever he spoke, and he was always ready to speak, at barbecues, commercial conventions, or political rallies, he sowed the seed of secession, but it was ten years before the seed would spring up and bear fruit.

By sheer rhetoric Yancey did more than anyone else in the South, more than Calhoun or Rhett, to prepare men's minds for the inevitability of secession. He was not a political philosopher, and he took no stock in Calhoun's elaborate scheme of concurrent majorities, whereby political decisions were arrived at not merely by counting heads but also by weighing the collective opinions of different classes or "interests." This "negative variation of the pressure group approach," as one of Calhoun's biographers has called it, made no headway with any of Calhoun's contemporaries. Any such attempt at redressing the balance against the South, Yancey considered a makeshift which did not reach to the heart of the problem. Two years in Congress, "a peep behind the scenes" as he described it, convinced him that the political leadership of the future would find its opportunity not in Washingon, but in the State conventions. Disgruntled with Congress, Yancey resigned and went home to begin a lonely and apparently hopeless campaign for Southern independence.

Although born in Warren County, Georgia, of old Virginia stock, Yancey received most of his education in the North. His father, a lawyer well respected in the community, died in 1817 leaving his widow with two young sons, William Lowndes aged three, and a baby, Benjamin Cudworth. Shortly after his death Mrs. Yancey remarried. Her second husband, the Rev. Nathan Beman, a Presbyterian schoolmaster, was teaching at Mt. Zion, Georgia, when he was called to Troy, New York, to become pastor there of the First Presbyterian Church. The family moved north in 1823 when William was eight years old, and the boy destined to be known as the most fanatical of Southern fire-eaters grew up and went to school and college in a purely Northern atmosphere. His stepfather, already a controversial figure in the church, plunged into the antislavery movement, and young William must have listened at the family dinner table to many a caustic comment on the South's "peculiar institution."

Just what effect Troy Academy and Williams College had upon him it is impossible to tell, but it is significant that during his two years at Williams, 1831-1833, he identified himself with the policies of Andrew Jackson rather than with those of Calhoun. In one of the college debates he was the leading speaker for the negative on the question, "Would the election of Andrew Jackson tend to destroy the Union?" The records show that he lost the debate, but he never lost his faith in Andrew Jackson or in the policies Jackson championed. Even on the issue of nullification, which made a disunionist of Rhett, Yancey stood squarely by the administration.

To the average Northerner nullification and secession amounted to about the same thing, but in Yancey's logical mind there was every difference. To secede from the Union seemed to him perfectly legitimate. The right of secession followed as a matter of course from the sovereignty of the States, otherwise why was so obvious an attribute of sovereignty not expressly renounced in the Constitution? Since the framers of the Constitution had deliberately rejected a proposal for the coercion of the States, the federal government clearly had no power to prevent secession. But to remain in the Union and nullify a federal law was quite another thing. Nullification would make the Union a rope of sand and place the government precisely in the position it occupied under the Articles of Confederation, when it had power to enact laws but no power to enforce them. The Constitution was clearly intended to enable the federal government to enforce obedience to her laws within those States belonging to the Union. Any State objecting to those laws was at liberty to secede.

Unfortunately for the South Yancey's logic, ingenious though it was, overlooked the hard fact that no such right as secession existed unless it could be enforced. The only sanction of revolution, as of legitimate government, is power. Lincoln, whose whole approach to politics was as practical as

Yancey's was theoretic, never lost sight of the essential element of power. On January 12, 1848, he made a speech in Congress opposing the Mexican War, which Southerners have often cited as justifying secession. "Any people anywhere," said Lincoln, "being inclined and having the power, have the right to rise up and shake off the existing government, and form a new one that suits them better. This is a most valuable, a most sacred right. . . ." The phrase "having the power" is easily missed, but it was thoroughly characteristic of Lincoln.

Homesick for the South and unwilling to be dependent on his stepfather, Yancey left college before graduation and entered the law office of Benjamin Perry, an old friend of his father's, in Greenville, South Carolina. Perry, a man of considerable importance who later became Governor of the State, was charmed by his young law student. Long after his death the Governor remembered him as "a man of deep feeling who spoke with extraordinary fluency and clearness of expression . . . he was the merriest of associates but when left to himself he was meditative to sadness." Although only just out of college Yancey seemed already to be blessed with all those qualities the South demands of its lawyers or its politicans. In a time of great political excitement in South Carolina, "he wielded a fierce and terrible pen against nullification." To Perry, a Unionist all his life, it must have seemed tragic that the man who opposed nullification so effectively in 1830 should have championed secession in 1860. He speaks of Yancey in his *Reminiscences* as the man to who more than anyone else is due "the awful responsibility of having applied the match which produced the bloody explosion." In spite of their differences of opinion, Perry's friendship with Yancey and Rhett was never interrupted.

The year after entering Perry's law office, Yancey married the daughter of a rich Greenville planter, Sarah Caroline Earle, and moved to a cotton plantation in Alabama. There he soon made a name for himself by the Yankee efficiency of his farming methods. The quiet life of a cotton planter was cut short by two "accidents" which throw a lurid light on Southern society. On one of his summer visits to Greenville Yancey became involved in a political argument with his wife's uncle, a certain Dr. Earle, who apparently lost his temper and attacked Yancey with a club. Unable to pacify him, Yancey drew a pistol and fired in self-defense. Dr. Earle fell, mortally wounded.

The case was tried in the circuit court in Greenville and the jury brought in a verdict of manslaughter. Yancey was sentenced to a $1,500 fine and twelve months' imprisonment, but the Governor, taking into consideration the prisoner's good character, released him from jail and remitted two-thirds of the fine. Shortly after his return to Alabama a second accident occurred, which proved to be the turning point of his career. Yancey had just bought another farm and was well on the way to becoming one of the most prosperous cotton planters in the State when his stock of slaves was almost entirely wiped out by poison. Unknown to him, a feud had broken out between his overseer and the overseer of the neighboring plantation. Such feuds were usually settled by a bowie knife, but in this case the neighboring overseer hit on what probably seemed to him a less dangerous method of dispatching his victim. He poisoned the spring which Yancey's overseer and Yancey's slaves were in the habit of using. The overseer survived but most of the slaves died in agony.

As a result of their death, the role of cotton planter which

Yancey had cut out for himself had to be abandoned. Realizing that his family and the few remaining invalid slaves would now have to be supported by his own efforts, he gave up farming and went back to the practice of law. He worked hard, friends rallied around him, and it was not long before he became one of the leading lawyers of Alabama. Success at the bar opened the way to politics, and at the age of twenty-seven he took his place in the lower house of the legislature as a States' rights Democrat of the strictest sect. Yancey did well enough in Alabama but when a by-election sent him to Congress he revealed his limitations. That he was one of the great orators of his generation no one denied. Chief Justice Stone, who shared none of Yancey's political opinions, thought him the greatest orator he had ever heard, but Yancey never mastered the art of working smoothly in party harness.

How irksome he found the daily wear and tear of political life is indicated by his controversy with Thomas Clingman, a Whig congressman from North Carolina. Clingman was one of the few Southerners who in the earlier part of his career upheld the right of Congress to regulate slave property in the Territories. In one of his speeches he criticized the policies of Calhoun with what seemed to Yancey unseemly bitterness, and Yancey had challenged him to a duel. Later on Clingman joined the forces of secession but in 1845, when the duel occurred, he was still a staunch Whig, eager for any compromise that would hold the Union together. Yancey had already left the rank and file of his own party far behind him, but he would not tolerate any criticism of it, particularly if the criticism reflected on the sanctity of slavery. There is something ironical in Clingman, a future brigadier in the Confederate army, charging Calhoun with pursuing a course

44

that would lead to the destruction of the Union, and in Yancey who did more than any other man to create the Southern Confederacy denying that Calhoun ever contemplated or desired anything so monstrous. The duel with Clingman ended bloodlessly. Yancey was said to have acquitted himself with scrupulous propriety, but the fact that he had killed one man in a family squabble, and fought a duel with another, was not easily forgotten. Times were changing and the South did not like to be reminded that Southern chivalry and Southern ruffianism sometimes merged into each other.

V

During his brief term in Congress, Yancey came in contact with many of the men whose names were to become household words to the next generation. With some of these new men, Stephen Douglas, Jefferson Davis and Alexander Stephens, he formed pleasant relationships, but he was never intimate with any of them. There was no bridge from his mind over to theirs. Unlike him they were still clutching at compromises, trying to preserve the balance between North and South, trying to hold the Democratic party together by directing attention to the importance of building a railroad across the continent, trying above all things to persuade the nation to stop talking about slavery.

In the years of controversy that lay ahead, Yancey had the immense advantage over other politicians of knowing his own mind. Like the abolitionists with whom he had so much in common, he stood foursquare before the world as the enemy of all compromise. He too could have said that he would not equivocate, that he would not retreat a single inch, and that he would be heard. The methods of Garrison and Yancey were different in that Garrison made his appeal through the printed word, while Yancey swayed the South from a rostrum by the magic of his voice, his wit and his impassioned logic. Not since the invention of printing has there ever been a society in which the orator counted for as much as he did in the Cotton Kingdom. Yancey set himself the task of loosening the bonds of affection that held the Union together by playing up the differences between the two sections of the country. No one would have suspected that his round, creaseless face marked the ardor of a Hebrew prophet, a prophet who was forever warning his people that if they compounded with the sins of free-soilers and abolitionists they would surely die.

The hundreds of addresses he made, sometimes lasting for three or four hours, were always carefully prepared. Nothing was left to the inspiration of the moment. A close-knit argument, founded on genuine grievances and seasoned with sarcasm, led his audiences step by step to the inevitability of secession. He told them that they had been too gullible in accepting Clay's famous Compromise, that it was a one-sided adjustment in which all the concessions were made by the South. The stocky, unromantic figure, and the conversational style of speaking, suggested the practical businessman rather than the uncompromising fanatic that Yancey really was. Men came away from his speeches believing, against their better judgment, that unless they were ready to submit to northern dictation they must fight for their independence just as their fathers had done in the Revolution. The theme of his speeches was always the same. Slavery was not an evil and,

46

unless the North was prepared to stop thinking of it as an evil, it would be better for all concerned if the two sections were to separate. It was not easy to square the conception of slavery as a paternal institution with the bloodcurdling picture, in the event of emancipation, of slaves murdering their masters and ravishing women, but the thousands who came to hear Yancey "give 'em hell" were not looking for inconsistencies. In the golden age of oratory, when speeches were not usually reprinted and when there were no lynx-eyed columnists ready to pounce on the unwary politician and confront him with what he had said the week before, an orator's chickens were not so likely to come home to roost.

Yancey's prediction that the Compromise would never settle the slavery question was fulfilled sooner than either he or the abolitionists had expected. The struggle broke out again in Congress with the introduction of bills organizing the Territories of Kansas and Nebraska. Was it the duty of the federal government to prohibit slavery in the Territories, or to maintain and protect it? Once again the fanatics on both sides trotted out the shop-worn arguments with which the nation was already so terribly familiar. The Yancey-Rhett thesis, borrowed from Calhoun, that the Constitution explicitly supported slavery in the Territories was of course wholly inadmissible in the North, while the opposite extreme, that slavery should never be allowed a foothold in the Territories, was equally inacceptable in the South.

It is ironic that it was an Illinois democrat, a man with no interest in promoting or arresting the spread of slavery, who quite unintentionally upset the delicate balance of the Compromise. The Northwest was destined to play an important role in the final break-up of the Union, and this was the first

47

move. Stephen Douglas was the most vigorous as well as the most colorful politician of his generation. A Vermonter by birth, he had gone west as a young man and identified himself with the fortunes of Illinois. Success had come easily to him. At twenty-eight years of age he was already a State supreme court judge, at thirty a congressman, at thirty-four a senator, and in 1852, when he was thirty-nine, he had narrowly missed the Democratic nomination for President. As an enthusiastic believer in the destinies of his country, an out-and-out expansionist who expected the United States to absorb the whole North American continent, Douglas was far more interested in the building of railroads, particularly a transcontinental railroad, than he was in the rights and wrongs of slavery.

By the middle of the century it was obvious that the two sides of the continent would soon be linked. The only question was which route the transcontinental railroad would take. Douglas suggested a railroad to the Pacific, passing through the Kansas–Nebraska Territory, with Chicago as its terminus, but before any such railroad could be built it would be necessary to organize a government in this Territory. Jefferson Davis, another expansionist, was already laying plans for what later became the Southern Pacific, and Senator Benton was agitating for a central route with the eastern terminal at St. Louis. Since no one expected that more than one railroad to the Pacific would ever be needed, Douglas knew that he would have to act quickly. His bill of January, 1854, was the answer. As a practical politician he knew that the organization of the Territory could be made possible only by Southern votes, and these votes would not be forthcoming unless Southern settlers were allowed to bring in their slaves.

The Kansas–Nebraska Act, for which Douglas was excoriated by the abolitionists and for which he got no thanks from the South, stated that the intent of the act was "not to legislate slavery into any Territory or State, nor to exclude it therefrom." Let the settlers in each Territory decide the issue for themselves. Surely that was sound democratic doctrine. Only by this system of "squatter sovereignty" could the Union continue to expand without being threatened by a crisis every time a new Territory was settled.

There was no reason to assume, as so many Northerners did, that slavery would move in bag and baggage unless specially interdicted by law. Douglas knew that slavery could not take root anywhere unless specially favored by soil and climate. Cotton had given it temporarily a new lease of life, but time was against it and eventually it would disappear. Where he failed as a statesman was in his inability to understand that the whole question was charged with emotion. The cynical honesty of his explanation of how slavery came to be abolished in Illinois was out of tune with the temper of the times. It jarred on the abolitionists, and it jarred no less on the slaveholders. "Why did our people," asked Douglas, "adopt a system of emancipation? Simply because they had ascertained, by experience, that with our climate, with our soil and our productions, slavery was not profitable. They could not make any money out of it, hence they turned philanthropist and abolished it."

Most Southerners, even extremists like Rhett and Yancey, must have known that slavery could not be transplanted into Kansas, but they were afraid of yielding a legal precedent which might later be used against them. At the same time Northerners, not trusting to nature, insisted that slavery be

49

formally condemned by the federal government. Essentially it was an academic struggle. As a Southern historian has expressed it: "The one side fought vigorously for what it was bound to get without fighting; the other, with equal rancor, contended for what it could never use."

In an effort to make his squatter sovereignty still more palatable to the South, Douglas was persuaded to add to his Kansas–Nebraska Bill a clause repealing the Missouri Compromise restriction. With the help of Jefferson Davis, at that time Secretary of War in President Pierce's Cabinet, the bill was finally passed on May 30, 1854, after months of angry debate. Henceforth immigrants from slave States, settling north of the line 36° 30′, could if they wished bring their live property with them. Once again Douglas thought he had acted as a statesman by placating the South without offering slaveholders anything to which a realistic abolitionist could object. Unfortunately the antislavery forces were not realistic. Instead of seeing that the hordes of Swedes and Germans who were pouring into the west, the small farmers from the Ohio valley and the New England enthusiasts, all of whom hated slavery, would easily outnumber the few Southerners willing to migrate with their slaves into a new country, they cursed Douglas for truckling to the slave interests.

Douglas's willingness to sponsor the repeal of the Missouri Compromise and thereby open the North to slavery convinced all those who disapproved of slavery, not just the little group who believed in immediate emancipation, that Douglas would sell his soul to win the Democratic nomination in the next campaign. That he would have liked to be President was certainly true, but it does not at all follow that in pressing for the repeal of the Missouri Compromise he deliberately surrendered his principles. Unlike the fanatics, North and South, he liked to think of himself as a realist, that is, a man who moved with the times. He would never have done anything to jeopardize the future of the white man in America, and that was as far as his principles extended. The excitement over slavery was something he never understood. He was not a man of fine feelings and, though he would have nothing to do with the institution himself, the mere fact of slavery did not offend him as it did Lincoln. His universe was bounded by material things, but he no more deserves obloquy on that account than do the politicians of today who are forever harping on "prosperity" and the "American way of life."

VI

Southern fanatics were no more satisfied with Douglas' gesture than the abolitionists. While the Northern press was thundering against him for trying "to exclude from a vast unoccupied region immigrants from the Old World and free laborers from our own States, and convert it into a dreary region of despotism inhabited by master and slaves," Yancey was attacking him no less vociferously for beguiling the South with bargains and promises. Nothing was to be gained, according to Yancey, by repealing the Missouri Compromise as long as a Territorial legislature was allowed to pass laws hostile to slavery. If the decision was to be based on numbers, the South had better surrender at once. In the struggle against the census returns, they would be beaten every time. By the time the Kansas–Nebraska Bill was signed, Yancey had made himself obnoxious to moderate men everywhere as the enemy of all compromise.

Douglas' triumph in getting his bill passed marked the low point in the political fortunes of the Southern fire-eaters. It seemed to prove what the great majority of Southerners had all along maintained—that slavery was not in danger. Was not the whole great West thrown open to the master and his slave? It was no good arguing that the ease with which a poor man could push on to the frontier with rifle and axe, compared with the encumbrances of the migrating slave-holders, made Douglas' famous squatter sovereignty little more than "a practical application of abolition objectives."

Rhett, Yancey and their ultra Southern friends must have wondered whether it would ever be possible to precipitate the South into revolution. The feeling for the Union was still so strong and the average Southerner was still so ready to be placated, so little aware of the dangers threatening him, that the fire-eaters must sometimes have despaired of whipping up that sense of intolerable injustice which drugs men into thinking they must fight in order to survive.

Unluckily for the South, at the moment when arguments for secession seemed to be failing, Fate was driving wedges of misunderstanding between the two sections which hotheads on both sides of the line were not slow to exploit. Unexpected allies in the shape of Harriet Beecher Stowe and John Brown provided the disunionists with just the ammunition they needed. As a weapon of propaganda *Uncle Tom's Cabin* is surely one of the great novels of all time. Never before had the slave been so idealized, or the slaveholder so bitterly re-viled. Mrs. Stowe implanted in the minds of millions of her readers at home and abroad, who had never given a thought to the subject before, the notion that the institution of slavery was inseparable from the most bestial cruelty. Uncle Tom became a world wide symbol of martyrdom. Reinforced by such popular poets as Longfellow and Whittier, the Northern press took up the cry where Mrs. Stowe had left off. Southern plantations, said the New York *Tribune*, "were little else than Negro harems."

The effect on the South of this barrage of abuse, and the recriminations that followed, was incalculable. Lincoln was not far wrong when on meeting Mrs. Stowe for the first time, in 1863, he addressed her as "the little woman who made the great war." Mrs. Stowe convinced Southerners, even those like Mary Boykin Chesnut, who hated slavery but did not know how to get rid of it, that the North had no solution to offer. As the wife of a United States Senator, the daughter of a Governor of South Carolina, and a very intelligent person in her own right, Mrs. Chesnut's observations on slavery are well worth contrasting with Harriet Beecher Stowe's. The fact that throughout the war she played the role of a Cassandra makes her comment on the activities of the abolitionists all the more tragic:

"On one side Mrs. Stowe, Greeley, Thoreau, Emerson, Sumner. They live in nice New England homes, clean, sweet-smelling, shut up in libraries, writing books which ease their hearts of their bitterness against us. What self-denial they do practice is to tell John Brown to come down here and cut our throats in Christ's name. Now consider what I have seen of my mother's life, my grandmother's, my mother-in-law's. These people were educated at Northern schools, they read the same books as their Northern contemporaries, the same daily papers, the same Bible. They have the same ideas of right and wrong, are high-bred, lovely, good, pious, doing their duty as they conceive it. They lived in Negro villages. They do not preach and teach hate as a gospel, and the sacred duty of murder and insurrection; but they strive to ameliorate the conditions of these Africans in every particular. They set them the example of a perfect life, a life of utter self-abnegation. Think of these holy New Englanders forced to have a Negro village walk through their houses whenever they see fit, dirty, slatternly, idle, ill-smelling by nature. These women I love have less chance to live their own lives in peace than if they were African missionaries. They have a swarm of blacks about them like children under their care, not as Mrs. Stowe's fancy painted them, and they hate slavery worse than Mrs. Stowe does. Book-making which leads you to a round of visits among crowned heads is an easier way to be a saint than martyrdom down here, doing unpleasant duty among the Negroes with no reward but the threat of John Brown hanging like a drawn sword over your head in this world, and threats of what is to come to you from blacker devils in the next."

The Charleston *Mercury* in the meantime took a savage satisfaction in reprinting from abolition papers all the bitterest comments on Southern life and Southern manners it could find. The inference to be drawn was obvious. How was it possible for the two sections of the country, feeling as they did toward each other, to go on living together as one nation? That was the rhetorical question Southern fanatics kept dinning into the ears of everyone within their reach. And yet Union sentiment was still so strong in spite of Seward's prophecy of an irrepressible conflict, in spite of the emotional effect of *Uncle Tom's Cabin*, the Fugitive Slave Law, the brutal assault on Sumner in the Senate, in spite finally of John Brown's attempt to stir up a slave insurrection, that it was not until Edmund Ruffin fired the first shot at Fort Sumter that the people of the United States could bring themselves to believe that they were deliberately plunging into war.

Of all the fantastic extremists on either side, Ruffin is the most interesting and the most tragic. A prophet without honor in his own State of Virginia, though he served it with the utmost devotion, he will be remembered in the North no less than in the South, long after the political issues of the day are forgotten, as the father of soil chemistry in America. In another age he would have had nothing to do with politics. As it was, John Brown and the abolitionists in general fired him with such a blind hatred of the North that at the end of the war, when the agonizing truth came home to him that the Confederacy had run its stormy course, he blew his brains out rather than live under Yankee domination.

Ruffin was essentially a dirt farmer, the first farmer in America to make a systematic study of the soil he worked. His essay on Calcareous Manures, in which he proved that the common fossil shells known as marl would correct the sterility of the soil, was called by a government expert, writing at the end of the nineteenth century, "the most thorough piece of work on an agricultural subject ever published in the English language."

In spite of his scientific interests, Ruffin was essentially a provincial, a Virginia farmer who knew nothing about the North except that it was inhabited by abolitionists and tight-fisted shopkeepers who believed in a high protective tariff, with whom the South had nothing in common. His Southern nationalism was a natural outgrowth of his absorption in farming. By restoring the fertility of the soil he hoped to check the stream of emigration westward, to stimulate the diversification of farming, and so make the South increasingly self-sufficient. Ruffin had no illusion about Kansas. He knew that the repeal of the Missouri Compromise meant nothing; that even if a pro-slavery constitution were foisted on Kansas or any other Territory, it would be reversed very soon by the arrival of new settlers. The only hope for the South of preserving its distinctive way of life lay not in competing with the North for new lands, but in breaking away from the North altogether.

Ruffin described himself in his diary as a "political outlaw bound or directed by no party allegiance, and knowing very little of party tactics or movements, so that my opinions were worth but little." But though that was true, Ruffin was more nearly right than Rhett or Yancey in realizing that the South could never be welded into a nation by speeches and newspaper articles. Independence involved rebuilding a ruined agricultural life. Cotton was not king, as so many Southern planters supposed. Only by reclaiming the soil, by giving up single crop production and by going back to general farming, could the South ever be prepared for a glorious independence. There could never be a united South as long as planters and farmers were forever drifting westward in search of new lands.

Along with his progressive views on farming went the usual acceptance of slavery as being in the best interest of the whites and of the Negro. Ruffin was quite aware that slavery was an expensive kind of labor, but the Negro was an inferior being incapable of self-direction. There was no future for the Negro in America other than slavery. He was a good master in that he looked after his slaves well and respected their family relations. It was because of his fear of emancipation, his conviction that the North was bent on destroying the only way of life he understood, that Ruffin became a rabid secessionist while so many of his friends in Virginia were still talking hopefully of a settlement of their difficulties.

So imbued was he with the importance of committing the South to complete independence that he urged Yancey to organize a "League of United Southerners" for just such a purpose. Ruffin had already reached the conclusion that the political parties had exhausted their usefulness. From now on patriots must learn to unite as Southerners rather than as Whigs or Democrats. He himself would gladly have undertaken the task if he had been blessed with Yancey's art of stirring a people, but he was no orator, and the South responded to oratory more readily than to his solemn array of statistics. Yancey threw himself into the scheme and began organizing all through the Southern States "Committees of Safety" devoted to fostering the idea of Southern independence. It was not as easy to get men to join these committees as Yancey had hoped. Southerners were too individualistic. They did not take kindly to the formation of pressure groups, which was what both he and Ruffin had in mind, and there were still too many areas of disagreement to permit of united action.

At the Southern Convention held in Montgomery, Alabama, in May, 1858, where Ruffin and Yancey had met and discussed the idea of a league of united Southerners, the fire-eaters had to face the fact that there were no issues except a common belief in slavery as a desirable state for the Negro (a belief shared by many Northerners as well) upon which the legislatures of the various Southern States could agree. South Carolina, for instance, would have welcomed free trade, whereas Louisiana, with an infant sugar industry to protect, would have opposed it. The Gulf States, still dreaming of expansion, flirted with the idea of reopening the slave trade, but any such proposal would have alienated Virginia and the Border States, where slavery was gradually petering out. Nor was there any general agreement on the ethics of the slave trade. The public conscience had been stirred by stories of the horrible cruelty of the "Middle Passage," but if slavery itself was a blessing and if it were admitted, as it surely had to be, that a Negro slave was better off in the Southern States than in the African jungle, who could argue that the trade was immoral? Rhett, Yancey and Ruffin were all at one moment in favor of reopening the trade on the grounds that the South could never be the homogeneous slave society it called itself until every white man in the South had a stake in the institution. Revival of the trade would increase the supply of slaves, lower the price, and thus put slave owning within the reach of everybody.

Their arguments, if you granted the premise, were brutally logical, but on the subject of slavery the American people, with the exception of a few fanatics, did not want to be logical. The average Southerner was ready enough to defend the institution, whether he owned a slave or not, but he shied away from defending the slave trade. The few extremists who demanded that the traffic be reopened finally gave way to the majority, on the theory that they must present a united front and not allow Northerners to know of the division in their ranks. Rhett continued to harp on the subject and, when the framers of the Confederate Constitution with supreme inconsistency repudiated the slave trade, he insisted, quite rightly, that they had placed a stigma on the whole institution. It was a question, thought Rhett, which should have been left for the individual States to decide for themselves. Even if it had been, the result would have been no different, since the fire-eaters were never able to commit a single State legislature to the reopening of the trade.

These disputes, many of them acrimonious, show what difficulties had to be overcome in persuading the Southern States to secede. The fire-eaters were always in the position of having to make bricks without straw. There were not enough issues around which everyone could rally. A few Southern Congressmen ranted about the underground railroad and fugitive slaves, but the handful of slaves who did escape came from the Border States, where secessionism was least popular. The census of 1860 shows that only 803 slaves escaped that year, which was approximately one fiftieth of one per cent of the total slaves in the country. As John G. Randall, the leading authority on Lincoln, said: "If the Civil War was fought because of fugitive slaves or on account of slavery in the West, the American people were miserably hoodwinked by the demon of strife."

The Charleston *Mercury* was still complaining in the spring of 1860 of "the contemptible policy which now characterizes a considerable portion of the South," meaning the willingness to give up the right of making Slave States out of the Territories, a right incidentally which it could not exercise. The slogan "No more Slave States," which the *Mercury* found so offensive, might be considered an insult but it was not an injury. The flow of population from the Northern States into the Territories had already settled the matter. It is one of the axioms of government that you must populate a country if you expect to govern it, and the South was never prepared to move out with its slaves into the Western Territories. Slaveholders might be attracted further to the south, but the Western plains held no charm for them. On the eve of Lincoln's inauguration there were only forty-six slaves in all the Territories of the United States—two in Kansas, fifteen in Nebraska, and twenty-nine in Utah, but for political purposes men talked about the extension of slavery into the Territories as if it were a real issue.

By the time the Democratic delegates met together in Charleston on April 23, 1860, to pick their candidate for President, the Rhetts, the Yanceys and the Ruffins were desperate. If the time were not ripe for a Southern Confederacy in 1860, it never would be. A tariff for the protection of industry might help them, but no one knew what sort of a tariff the Republicans would enact. In any case no State, except possibly South Carolina, could be induced to secede merely because of a protective tariff. As for Congressional approval of slavery in the Territories, most Southerners were beginning to realize that there was no remaining federal territory where conditions were favorable to slavery. Douglas was talking about burying Southern disunionism and Northern abolitionism in the same grave, which was precisely what the fanatics were determined to prevent. A harmonious convention, ending in the nomination of Douglas, might well lead to a democratic victory in the fall, in which case the South would never secede.

Only if a black Republican were elected, preferably Seward, would there be any hope of persuading the Southern States to take the plunge. But first, they must wreck the Democratic party, for as long as that remained intact their dream could never be fulfilled. Wrecking the party involved requiring of two-thirds of the members present positive approval of the institution of slavery and of its extension into the Territories. The work of demolition was entrusted to Yancey, and he did it with consummate skill. Alexander Stephens, whose heart was never in the Confederacy though he became its vice-president, believed that Rhett and Yancey intended from the beginning "to rule or ruin." The proceedings of the Charleston convention prove how right he was.

VII

The convention was hardly under way before Union Democrats were wondering what they were doing in Charleston. The Northern delegates in particular could not help noticing the contrast between the charming eighteenth century houses half hidden behind wrought iron gates, and the rest of the city. "There are many large imposing houses," wrote an English traveller of the period, "with pillars and verandahs, no doubt the residences of the aristocratic Southerners; the rest of the habitations are small and poor-looking. There seems no middle class; only rich and poor." A delegate from some raw but thriving community in the Northwest must have eyed his fellow Democrats from the South with a good deal of curiosity. The slave markets where the human merchandise was exposed for sale were even more unreal than the porticoed houses. This was an alien world with which he had nothing in common.

There was only one man, Stephen Douglas, capable of meeting the challenge of the lusty young Republican party by bridging the gulf between Northern and Southern Democrats. Would the Cotton States accept his severely neutral position on slavery, or would they insist on a candidate and a platform more representative of their own extreme views? On that issue hung the very life of the party. Douglas was supremely confident. Not for nothing was this miniature gladiator, with a lionlike head and a deep bass voice, known as the "Little Giant." Though he stood only five feet, two inches tall, he was the very essence of combativeness. For the last ten years Douglas had been fighting on two fronts, but no one, not even the long-legged lawyer with whom he had been barnstorming up and down the State of Illinois, had shaken his belief in the marvelous efficacy of squatter sovereignty.

This doctrine, ridiculed by Lincoln as sacrificing everything to the slave interests, was damned by Yancey for the very opposite reason, that it conceded too much to the abolitionists. The cotton planters, taking their cue from Rhett and Yancey, refused to have anything to do with Douglas' famous panacea. In the lobbies of the Charleston and Planters' hotels, they talked truculently about the positive virtues of slavery. They never understood that the slave system, apparently so firmly entrenched, was bound to pass away, and that their real interests called for the policy of gradual adjustment that Douglas offered them. They had talked themselves into thinking of slavery as something to be proud of, something that Congress was in honor bound to maintain, protect and expand.

The struggle in the convention focused on the wording of the platform. After a week of bitter discussion, two reports were submitted. The majority report, signed by the fifteen slave States, demanded government protection for slaveholders and denied the right of either Congress or a territorial legislature to prohibit slavery in a Territory. Any assumption, direct or indirect, that a lawgiver could in any way discriminate against slave property, was not only mistaken but insulting to slaveholders. The delegates from the Free States, eager to conciliate their Southern brethren but not to the extent of antagonizing their own people, brought in a minority report in which they skirted the issue of slavery in the Territories and declared that the party would abide by the decisions of the Supreme Court.

The stage was now set for Yancey. This was his great moment. As the smiling, squat figure rose up to speak, the Northern delegates braced themselves for the attack. Unlike the preacher described by Lincoln, who looked as if he were fighting bees, Yancey stood perfectly still. He made none of the theatrical gestures which were the stock in trade of most Southern orators. The *New York Times* described him as "a clear, cool, straightforward speaker, methodical in argument, precise in language. . . ." Ruffin, who envied Yancey his ability to sway an audience, was not always pleased by his speeches. Sometimes he found him "too wordy and too long," sometimes the aroma of whisky was too strong, but on this occasion he appears to have been at his best. For an hour and a half, he reviewed the controversy over slavery. Finally, as it grew dark, he turned to the Northern delegates in the flickering light of the gas lamps and reminded them, still in the same mellifluous voice, that the fault was all theirs, that if they would only learn to interpret the Constitution literally, as their comrades in the South did, there would be no more discord within the Democratic party.

Was slavery right or wrong? After all, that was the issue, the issue Douglas wanted to evade because it led only to barren controversy, and that Yancey and Lincoln, attacking him from opposite sides, were determined that he should face. It was the rock upon which the Democratic party finally split, as the Southern fanatics were determined that it should. Hardly had Yancey sat down before Senator Pugh of Ohio was on his feet. The Northern delegates, he assured Yancey, would never put themselves on record as endorsing slavery and recommending its extension. "Gentlemen of the South," he exclaimed, "you mistake us—you mistake us—we will not do it."

The debate could go on no further. Realizing that they had reached a dead end, the delegates voted to adjourn. The rest of the proceedings were an anticlimax. Though Douglas could still count on a substantial block of Northern delegates, a longstanding feud with President Buchanan, combined with the uncompromising hostility of the Southerners, prevented his ever reaching the necessary two-thirds majority. No doubt Yancey did not represent the point of view of all the delegates who opposed Douglas. Jefferson Davis, for example, and John Slidell, neither of whom could yet be described as out-and-out secessionists, were among the friends of Buchanan who wanted to defeat Douglas and carry the election to the House, where they thought there was a better chance of electing a Democrat than in the electoral college.

The Douglas forces, though they were not strong enough to win the nomination, managed to defeat the report of the program committee sponsored so eloquently and so disastrously by Yancey, and to adopt the innocuous minority platform. The Alabama delegation led by Yancey then left the hall, followed by most of the delegations from the other Cotton States. As a result of this split in the party two Democratic candidates were eventually nominated—Douglas on a squatter sovereignty platform, and John C. Breckinridge, Buchanan's

vice-president, on a platform that specifically advocated federal protection of slavery in the Territories. The Border
States, disgusted with both wings of the party, nominated
John Bell of Tennessee to carry the banner of a new party,
the Congressional Union party, which pledged itself to stick
its head in the sand, in other words to avoid the distracting
issue of slavery altogether.

Yancey played an important part in the nomination of
Breckinridge, but his real contribution to history had already
been made. By persuading the Cotton States to adopt a "no
compromise" stand at Charleston, he forced them into a position where there was virtually no alternative to secession.
Even so there were many reluctant secessionists in the South
who never quite realized what they were doing when they
followed Yancey into the wilderness. The point has often
been made that the break-up of the Democratic party in 1860
made no difference in the Presidential election. On the basis
of the electoral votes, Lincoln would have been President
anyway. It is of course a fact that Lincoln received more electoral votes than Douglas, Breckinridge and Bell all put together but, if the Democratic party had not been split, surely
it is possible that many of the Lincoln votes would have gone
to Douglas. The bandwagon was no less operative in 1860 than
it is today, and there must have been many Democrats who
stayed away from the polls or voted for Lincoln rather than
record their votes for a man who had no chance of being
elected.

During the presidential campaign of 1860, Yancey, as if he
realized his mistake, made an oratorical tour of the North,
speaking to packed audiences in New York, Boston and many
other places in a belated attempt to stem the Lincoln tide. The

New York Times, while disagreeing with the main theme of his argument, that "slavery must cease to be regarded as an evil and the whole conduct of the Government must proceed on the opposite assumption," complimented him on the good temper of his remarks. (October 11, 1860) Again and again during his speeches, hecklers demanded of Yancey what he would do if Lincoln were elected. "We cannot resist the inauguration of Lincoln," answered Yancey, "conducted according to the forms of law. . . . But there remains the right of self-preservation. This does not involve the right to injure others. It is the right to save ourselves from despotism and destruction—the right to withdraw ourselves from a government which endeavors to crush us."

Once again, as in the nullification days, Yancey reveled in distinctions that made no difference. He would not oppose Lincoln, yet he would secede. He had good reason to believe that the action of any State will be peaceable, that "it will not be resisted under the present or any probable administration of public affairs."

It is characteristic of fanatics to be so intoxicated by their own logic as to ignore the evidence on the other side. Yancey, Rhett and Ruffin convinced themselves, as did their opposite numbers in the North, that the two sections had come to the parting of the ways, and that the separation would take place without bloodshed. In their defense it may be said that better men than they had made the same mistake. Long before 1860 John Quincy Adams, in a speech on the fiftieth anniversary of Washington's inauguration, had faced and accepted the possibility of peaceful secession. "If the day should ever come (may Heaven avert it)," said Adams, "when the affection of the people of these states shall be alienated from each other . . .

66

far better will it be for the people of the disunited states to part in friendship from each other than to be held together by constraint." Immediately after Lincoln's election, and before South Carolina had passed its secession ordinance, the New York *Tribune*, a staunchly Republican paper, insisted over and over again that a Union pinned together by bayonets was out of the question. (1860. November 9, 16, 23) General Winfield Scott, the ranking general in the United States army, wrote to Seward urging him to "let the wayward sisters depart in peace." Former President Franklin Pierce, to cite but one more example of peace at any price, seriously maintained that under the circumstances no wise man would dream of coercion. The reluctance of the South to secede, and of the North to accept the challenge of secession, convinced a naturally optimistic public that there would be no war.

Even after South Carolina had voted herself out of the Union, the fanatics still had their work cut out for them. Responsible papers in the South continued to advocate a "wait and see" policy.

The Republican party platform expressly denied any intention of interfering with slavery where it already existed, so that it was necessary to prove, by quoting from the speeches and writings of abolitionists, that whatever the party platform might say the Lincoln supporters clearly contemplated the extinction of slavery throughout the Union. By the end of 1860, extremists had so manipulated the minds of the voters that few men were in a position to think, speak and act for themselves. Lincoln himself remained inexplicably silent. On the mistaken theory that his views were well known, though they were not known in the South at all, he said nothing between the Cooper Union speech in February, 1860, and the

First Inaugural in March, 1861, to dispell the fears of Union-loving slaveholders as to what the election of a "black Republican" really meant. With the moderate men unable or unwilling to make themselves heard, it was natural enough that the fanatics should have taken things into their own hands. By playing up the "higher law" and the "house divided" speeches of Seward and Lincoln, they finally began winning converts to the belief that the South had reached the end of the road. When a higher law than the Constitution is invoked on one side, it is not surprising that revolutions should be foreshadowed on the other. "The tea has been thrown over board," declared the Charleston *Mercury* on November 7, 1860, "the Revolution of 1860 has been initiated."

In the same issue the *Mercury* reprinted articles from Boston papers about the readiness of the Southern people to applaud threats of disunion, and their unwillingness to act on them. James Russell Lowell, on the very eve of the election in 1860, was assuring his countrymen that the Union was not in danger. "Mr. W. L. Yancey, to be sure, threatens to secede; but the country can get along without him, and we wish him a prosperous career in foreign parts. . . . That gentleman's throwing a solitary somerset will hardly turn the continent head over heels."

Lowell's irony shows how little even intelligent observers realized how close to the edge of the precipice they were. Rhett maintained that if South Carolina did not secede on or before the inauguration of President Lincoln, a "black Republican" who had not won a single vote in any of the Cotton States, she would become the laughing stock of the whole world. This was his answer to those, like Jefferson Davis and Alexander Stephens, who, though they believed as deeply as he did in the right of secession, were always waiting for some overt act on the part of the Republicans that would unite the whole South against them. Stephens still insisted that Lincoln was not a bad man, and that the situation had not yet reached the breaking point.

The election of Lincoln was the signal for increased activity among the compromisers. Maybe secession was inevitable, but they must keep putting off the evil day as long as possible. Above all, the Southern States must not dribble into secession one by one. They must all hang together or they would hang separately. This was just the opposite of the fire-eaters' point of view. Unless some one was prepared to take the lead, the whole movement for secession would peter out again, just as it had in 1833 and in 1850.

Rhett knew that South Carolina must assert her leadership now or never, and that she must be carried out of the Union while resentment over the election was at its height Fortunately for him, the presidential electors in South Carolina were chosen by the State legislature instead of by popular vote as in the other States. If the whole people of South Carolina had voted, the result might well have been different. After casting the State's vote unanimously for Breckinridge, the legislature remained in session to learn the outcome of the election. On November 9, as soon as the news of Lincoln's victory had been received, a bill was passed calling for a secession convention to meet on January 15. Even then Rhett was not satisfied. The delay of a whole month would play into the hands of those who believed in the necessity of joint action by all the Southern States. Once again he rallied his forces to advance the date of the Convention.

This time there was no stopping him. Minute men carefully

schooled in advance agitated for quick action. An inflammatory telegram reached Charleston on November 9 announcing that Robert Toombs had resigned as United States Senator from Georgia, and that the Governor of Georgia had recommended the immediate calling of a convention to consider secession. The news about Senator Toombs happened to be false, but it coincided with the resignation in Charleston of a popular federal judge, Andrew G. Magrath. Mrs. Chesnut noted in her diary that pictures of the judge "in the frightfullest signpost-style of painting were suspended across various streets in Charleston. The happy moment seized by the painter to depict him was while Magrath was in the act of dramatically tearing off his robes of office in rage and disgust at Lincoln's election. . . . He is depicted with a countenance flaming with contending emotions—rage, disgust and disdain." Everywhere the Stars and Stripes were coming down, and the palmetto flags were going up.

For the moment the conservatives were paralyzed. No one could stand out against the drumfire of Rhett's propaganda. The legislature reversed itself, called the Convention a month earlier than had been intended, and on December 20, 1860, the *Mercury* proclaimed to the world, "The Union is dissolved." Within the next six weeks the flames of secession engulfed Mississippi, Florida, Alabama, Georgia, Louisiana and Texas. Rhett's dream had come true. South Carolina had raised the flag of independence, and the Cotton States had rallied round her. Lincoln announced that the crisis had been "gotten up . . . by designing politicians," which was true enough, but the gentle remedy he proposed—"keeping cool" —showed how far he was from appreciating the magnitude of the task ahead.

VIII

For the first time in their lives, Rhett and Yancey knew what it was to be in tune with the times, but the bewildering sensation of popularity did not last. By the time the delegates from the Cotton States met at Montgomery to form a Southern Confederacy, the control of affairs had passed into the hands of the more reluctant and more realistic secessionists. Revolutions are usually initiated by men who demand only moderate reforms, which the existing government is too blind to concede. Gradually fanatics get control, and the more moderate reformers are ousted. In the case of the Confederacy, the normal procedure was reversed. It was the fanatics who initiated the movement of secession, but in the moment of their triumph they were discarded in favor of those whom they had had to goad into action.

In the new government, the fanatics were deliberately ignored. Rhett coveted the presidency for himself and, failing that, hoped to be offered the post of Secretary of State, or that of commissioner to England, on one or the other of which he had staked all his hopes. He was passed over in favor of men whom he suspected of still being Unionists at heart. Yancey was not even chosen as a delegate owing to a curious ordinance which did not permit members of the Alabama State Convention to serve in the new "national" convention as well. In any case his day of usefulness to the cause, like Rhett's, was over. The Confederacy needed trained administrators rather than orators and agitators, and Yancey was not an administrator. He enjoyed one last moment of intoxicating applause when, as chief of the reception committee, he pre-

71

sented the new President to the wildly cheering crowd assembled to greet him. Fully conscious that they were making history, the citizens of Montgomery had selected for the occasion the greatest orator in the land. Under the glow of his eloquence, the few remaining doubting Thomases were transformed into ardent apostles. Yancey reminded the delegates that theirs was the most sacred trust. A new nation was being born. "Gentlemen," he exclaimed, as he presented Jefferson Davis to them, "the hour and the man have met."

Never again would the President of the Confederacy bask in the warmth of such applause. For the moment, but only for the moment, the South took him to her heart as the beau ideal of the soldier statesman, the new George Washington under whose banner they would re-establish their independence. Years after the Confederacy had crumbled, men still recalled the thrill of patriotism Yancey's words had inspired.

In many ways the friends of Jefferson Davis were fully justified in thinking that the Confederacy had chosen an altogether exceptional man as President. Davis had already given proof of his gallantry in the field, in the Mexican War, and of his administrative ability in the Cabinet, as President Pierce's Secretary of War. He was well-educated, fearlessly honest, a good public speaker and a tireless worker, but he knew nothing of the ways of politicians, and he was too conscious of his own rectitude to care to learn them. Lincoln's knack of getting men of widely different views to work for him was left out of Jefferson Davis. He persisted in thinking that anyone who criticized his policies must be either stupid or malicious. Although dignified and courteous by nature, the terrific headaches to which he was subject often made him cross and petulant. Mrs. Davis speaks of his coming home from the office "a mass of throbbing nerves." That he and the fanatics should have grated upon each other was not surprising.

The disappointment of Rhett and Yancey at not being consulted by the President colored their whole attitude toward the Confederate government. Their doubts about Jefferson Davis' judgment soon developed into dislike, amounting almost to hatred, of the man himself. The Charleston *Mercury* began sniping at the new President before he had been in office a month. All his appointments were bad, since most of those selected for office had been former co-operationists. The fact was that a great many of the Southerners who were to distinguish themselves under the Confederacy, including Robert E. Lee, opposed secession during the hectic crisis of 1860-61, and the fanatics could never bring themselves to believe that such reluctant secessionists deserved as much consideration as those, like themselves, who had been preaching the doctrine for thirty years. Jefferson Davis was reported to have shed tears on retiring from the United States Senate. Alexander Stephens had actually spoken favorably of Lincoln, and had expressed regret that the South had forced the issue at Charleston in 1860. Even Robert Toombs of Georgia, who was more of a secessionist than most, voted against the firing on Fort Sumter on the ground that it would lose the South every friend in the North. What could be expected of such half-hearted rebels?

Rhett and Yancey were particularly disgusted by the foreign policy of the Confederacy. It seemed to them hopelessly shortsighted. Davis, anxious no doubt to get rid of Yancey, sent him to Europe as chairman of a commission to treat with the great powers for recognition of the Confederate States, but he was given no special instructions and no power to act. Unless the Confederate government were willing to offer substantial commercial advantages, Yancey saw clearly that the commission would be wasting its time. It would require a very tempting bait indeed to induce the British government to run counter to the widespread antislavery feeling of its people by recognizing a new nation whose whole economy was founded on slavery. Rhett, as chairman of the committee on foreign relations in the provisional government, drew up a plan offering England a practical monopoly of trade with the Confederacy for the next twenty years, but Davis was too good an American to accept dependence on England as the price of separation from the North. He preferred to assume that the Confederate States could deal on equal terms with foreign nations and that, if the foreign nations were not at first friendly, King Cotton would soon bring them to heel. It was beneath his dignity to offer bribes or gifts. Rhett argued that without the backing of England the Confederacy would never establish its independence, just as in the days of the Revolution the thirteen colonies would never have become a nation without the help of France, but Davis brushed him aside. He was always too busy to listen to people who did not agree with him.

As the war dragged on there were many ardent secessionists besides Rhett and Yancey who came to believe that everything Jefferson Davis did was wrong. They criticized him for trying to impose his will on sovereign independent States. Those who complained at the time of his election that he was not a thorough-going secessionist ended by distrusting him still more for assuming the role of a dictator. Apparently it never occurred to Rhett or to any other devotees of States' rights that the Confederacy contained within itself the seeds of decay. The eagerness of the Charleston authorities to take possession of Fort Sumter presented the Montgomery government with a foretaste of the difficulties that lay ahead. The Confederate Congress resolved to take under its charge the whole question of the occupation of the forts, but this was done under the protest of South Carolina. Governor Pickens informed the Congress that they were asserting rights that did not belong to them.

The exigencies of war often compelled Jefferson Davis, just as they compelled Lincoln, to take over powers not expressly assigned to him by the Constitution, but Lincoln could always claim that he was acting in defense of the Union whereas, in defending the Confederacy, Davis was forever haunted by the specter of States' rights. In defending the one he must sacrifice the other. It was ironical but inevitable that the men who declaimed most vehemently against the injustice of the Washington government, and had been the first to advocate secession as the only remedy for their wrongs, were also among the first to accuse Davis of despotism.

Yancey actually stated in the Confederate Senate that he preferred a Northern conquest to a Davis despotism. By the end of the war, it seemed almost as if the Confederacy were being kept alive not by the government in Richmond but by the Army of the Potomac. In the presence of the enemy, Southerners closed their ranks, forgot their differences and died rather than let the enemy pass, but the disease in the body politic was there and it was incurable.

Lincoln, with his usual insight, put his finger on this inherent weakness in the Confederacy. He pointed out, in his First

Inaugural Address, that if a minority insists on seceding when it is outvoted, "they make a precedent which in turn will divide and ruin them; for a minority of their own will secede from them whenever a majority refuses to be controlled by such minority." As Lincoln had predicted, the Southern States remained as incapable of co-ordinated action after secession as they had been before. Whether the Union armies hastened or delayed the collapse of the Confederacy is open to question.

Rhett found himself more in sympathy with men like Governor Brown of Georgia and Zebulon Vance of North Carolina, both of whom he would have called half-hearted secessionists in 1860, than with the Confederate government. These men were ready to co-operate with the other States in the Confederacy when it suited them, but they would not take orders from Richmond any more than they would take orders from Washington. The State of North Carolina operated its own blockade runners with conspicuous success, but whatever came through the blockade was destined for the use of its own troops and was not put at the disposal of the government. By the end of the war, when Lee's tattered and starving army was desperately defending Petersburg and Richmond, Governor Vance had accumulated in the warehouses of Wilmington a surplus of 92,000 uniforms and 150,000 pounds of bacon.

Whether or not Rhett realized it, such conditions were inherent in the vast slave empire of independent States of which he had always dreamed. In the final collapse of the Confederacy, he remained convinced of the wisdom of his own statesmanship and the needless folly of others. Though secession had brought to his countrymen unutterable misery instead of the peace and prosperity he had prophesied, though he was ruined by the war like everybody else, his faith in God and in the rightness of his cause enabled him to live out the rest of his life in a strange unworldly serenity.

John Bigelow, when he visited Charleston for the first time, in 1867, was delighted to find a member of the Rhett family driving a streetcar. The family had done so much harm in the world, thought Bigelow, that he was pleased to see one of them at last doing something useful. It was perhaps a natural reaction in view of the fact that in 1860 Barnwell Rhett Jr. had threatened to tar and feather any reporter from the N. Y. *Evening Post*, the Bigelow paper, who came south to report the proceedings of the secession convention. But whatever satisfaction Bigelow may have taken in the downfall of the Rhett family, he would have been disappointed to find Rhett himself quite unchanged.

Rhett died in 1876 without ever having applied for a pardon from the federal government, and without ever losing faith in the destiny of the South. That he had failed, or rather that Jefferson Davis had failed, was unimportant. Posterity would vindicate him. Like all fanatics, he developed an armor against reality which mere fact could not penetrate. His passion for State sovereignty was incompatible with his belief in Southern independence, his vision of a mighty slave empire teeming with poets and philosophers was a mirage, but four years of war ending with the crushing defeat of all his hopes left him still happily convinced that in God's good time North and South would have to follow the course that he had charted.

Yancey was the only one of the fire-eaters to be spared the ignominy of defeat, but the last years of his life were far from happy. He returned to his beloved Aabama early in 1862, deeply discouraged by his experience abroad. He was sick in body as well as in mind. Mason and Slidell, who headed the next commission to Europe, proved equally unsuccessful. For one moment it looked as if Captain Wilkes's high-handed action in removing the new commissioners from a British ship would lead to war between Britain and the United States, and Southern hopes rose accordingly, but at the last minute Seward yielded to British pressure, and Mason and Slidell were surrendered. Though the incident left bitter feelings in the North, it did not profit the South. In London, the *Times* admitted that Mason and Slidell were "about the most worthless booty it would be possible to extract from the jaws of the American lion." (January 11, 1862)

Yancey fell foul of the government as soon as he got home by speaking out openly about the hopelessness of counting on foreign intervention. His relations with Jefferson Davis grew steadily worse. During his absence in England, he had been elected to the Confederate Senate, and it was not long before he had joined forces with all those who were criticizing Davis for ignoring the rights of the individual states. Lincoln's question, "Must a government, of necessity, be too strong for the liberties of its own people, or too weak to maintain its own existence?" was one that no Confederate, least of all Rhett or Yancey, cared to face.

In the last few months of his life he became more and more convinced that the Confederacy was in deadly peril, not so much from the Northern armies as from the ineptitude of

Davis himself and the little clique of second-rate men by whom he was surrounded. He died in the summer of 1863, a few weeks before the battle of Gettysburg, still believing, as the epitaph on his gravestone records, that he was justified of all his deeds.

Yancey was one of those dangerous men who, because they so obviously believe every word they say, compel the allegiance of weaker spirits. And yet, in spite of all their eloquence and sincerity, Yancey, Rhett and Ruffin, and their little cohort of "no-compromisers," could never by themselves have precipitated the war. The American people were no less disposed to peace in 1860 than they are today. Seward was perfectly correct in believing that up to and even after the firing on Fort Sumter there were rumblings of Unionist sentiment to be heard all through the South. Even in South Carolina, Rhett felt that the enthusiasm for secession would evaporate unless Sumter were attacked. It was significant that no one wanted to fire the first shot. Roger Pryor, a Virginia secessionist, declared to an enthusiastic audience in Charleston that in case of conflict Virginia would secede "within an hour by Shrewsbury clock," but when the Charleston gentlemen offered him the honor of pulling the lanyard that would send the first shell on its way, he drew back and said, "I don't want to begin the war."

That dubious honor fell to Edmund Ruffin, who was "highly gratified by the compliment, and delighted to perform the service." He hoped that the "bloodshed of South Carolinians defending their soil and their rights . . . will stir doubly fast the sluggish blood of the more backward Southern States into secession and intimate alliance." The sense of urgency is always there. It was as if Ruffin knew that unless some decisive action were taken to establish its prestige, the Confederacy would crumble to pieces. There were radicals in the North, too, who were equally delighted at the prospect of bloodshed. Senator Chandler of Michigan had no patience with those who still talked of negotiating with the South. Without a little bloodletting the Union, in Chandler's estimation, will not "be worth a rush." The mammoth petitions signed by 22,000 persons in Massachusetts urging Congress to adopt the Crittenden Compromise had filled him with horror.

Unfortunately every time the levelheaded people in the South seemed about to assert themselves, a John Brown, a Sumner, a Garrison or a Wendell Phillips could be counted on to demand immediate emancipation, and to whip up fears of slave insurrections, to which the Rhett-Yancey insistence on Southern independence seemed to be the only answer. Secession might still have been averted if all these men had not been so utterly convinced they were right. They pointed out with some show of reason that the conflict was, as Seward had said, irrepressible, and that the sooner it came the better. Actually, if the conflict was irrepressible it was only because, for the first time in American history, policy was being dictated by irresponsible fanatics and not at all because the issues involved admitted of no solution.

In the crisis of 1860 time, good will and common sense, the three essential factors in the maintenance of peace, were all lacking. The fanatics had been balked before. This time there would be no mistake. With disastrous ingenuity they had succeeded in arousing throughout the nation, in the North as well as in the South, a sense of intolerable injustice. The American people are traditionally slow to anger but, when the consciousness of evil is brought home to them, and when they face the alternatives of peace or war, they have invariably chosen the harder way.

TWO

The Abolitionists

I

IN ONE of the last speeches of his life, John C. Calhoun predicted that, unless it were put a stop to, "the long continued agitation of the slave question on the part of the North" would end in disunion. As the originator of the strange doctrine of nullification, no one knew better than Calhoun that economic issues had also played a part in producing the sectional pattern that alienated the South from the North. It was no doubt true that the South believed itself to be, in Rhett's words, "the very best colony . . . that any country ever had," but the galling truth that the South needed Northern capital to finance the growing of its staple crops, Northern commission agents to market them, and Northern vessels to carry its exports and imports, was not enough of itself to create a demand for political independence. After all, Northern businessmen, however smart they might appear, owed their livelihood to King Cotton no less than did the Southern planters. The economy of the South had certainly evolved in a very different way from the economy of the North, but those differences need not necessarily have led to war.

It was not even slavery but rather, as Calhoun put it, "the ceaseless agitation over slavery" that made the conflict irrepressible. As long as the "peculiar institution" could be dealt with as a constitutional, an economic, or a political issue, as it had been in the early days of the republic, there was always room for give and take. Only when the abolitionists succeeded in winning over the North to their view of slavery as a sin did the hopes of any lasting compromise begin to fade. Peace invariably flies out of the window whenever morality thrusts itself into a quarrel. So it was in America a hundred years ago.

Historians have often pointed out that down to the very end, and even after the firing on Sumter, the abolitionists remained a small and unpopular minority, denounced not only by the South, but by conservative opinion throughout the Union, as dangerous fanatics. No political leader of national importance ever committed himself wholeheartedly to the support of abolitionist doctrines. Undoubtedly this is true, just as it is true that no Southern politician of any standing ever publicly endorsed the policies of Rhett and Yancey. As late as 1858, Jefferson Davis was comparing secessionists to "mosquitoes around the horns of an ox, who could annoy but could do no harm." And yet Calhoun was right in insisting that the agitation over slavery in the North, and the inevitable reaction to that agitation in the South, created a fog of misunderstanding in which the rank and file of the American people lost touch with each other, and in which nothing could be heard but the angry recriminations of men and women who had sworn never to compromise.

Chief among the no-compromisers, at least in the eyes of the South, was William Lloyd Garrison, the most widely known but by no means the first or the most effective of the abolitionists. Strangely enough it was not Garrison's Northern supporters, but his Southern enemies, who made him famous.

If a Southern slaveholder had been asked at any time during the eighteen-thirties who was the most wicked man in America, the name of Garrison would immediately have jumped to his mind. As the founder of the *Liberator*, a weekly journal dedicated to the cause of immediate emancipation, he was held directly responsible for the Nat Turner slave insurrection, in the course of which some fifty white persons, men, women and children, were murdered. In commenting on the insurrection, Garrison said, "If we would not see our land deluged in blood, we must immediately burst the shackles of the slaves." There is no evidence that Nat Turner ever saw a copy of the *Liberator*, but the South continued to believe that Garrison, who actually hated violence in any form, was bent on fomenting wars between the slaves and their masters.

In the very first number of the *Liberator*, Garrison proclaimed to the world that on the subject of slavery "I do not wish to think, or speak, or write, with moderation. No! No! Tell a man whose house is on fire to give a moderate alarm; tell him to moderately rescue his wife from the hands of the ravisher; tell the mother to gradually extricate her babe from the fire into which it has fallen;—but urge me not to use moderation in a cause like the present. I am in earnest—I will not equivocate—I will not excuse—I will not retreat a single inch—AND I WILL BE HEARD." Some editor in the South got hold of this copy of the *Liberator* and it was widely quoted in the Southern press. Garrison, who so far was known in New England only as one of the innumerable small town reformers, woke up to find himself infamous. So widespread was the feeling against him in the South that the legislature of Georgia, in 1831, appropriated five thousand dollars to be paid by the Governor "to any person or persons who shall arrest, bring to trial and prosecute to conviction, under the laws of the State, the editor or publisher of a certain paper called the *Liberator*, published in the town of Boston and the State of Massachusetts."

Garrison had enough of the Old Testament prophet in him to rejoice in the fear and hatred he inspired. The son of a Nova Scotia sea captain who had moved to Newburyport, where he deserted his wife because she nagged at him for drinking, young Garrison's early history is the familiar story of the poverty-stricken boy who triumphs over his environment. His father dropped out of his life while he was still an infant and was never heard from again, but his mother adored him and did everything within her power to fill his father's place. Unfortunately there was no money to provide the education for him she would have liked and, at the age of nine, young Lloyd had to be apprenticed to a shoemaker. The boy lived with his employer and was well treated, but for Mrs. Garrison, who dreamed of better things for her son, it was a hard decision. When the shoemaker moved to Baltimore, Mrs. Garrison and her two sons decided to go too. Apparently the business did not prosper. The older boy James, a ne'er-do-well like his father, ran away to sea, while Lloyd, who loved his mother but found her as difficult to get along with as everybody else did, persuaded her to let him return to Newburyport. She must have been able to pay something toward his keep for he boarded with a Baptist deacon and attended the local grammar school, but only for a few months. By the time he was thirteen he had started on another apprenticeship, this time to a cabinetmaker, but carpentering proved no more to his taste than shoemaking. He ran away from his employer, a serious offense in those days which might well have landed him in jail if the cabinetmaker, sensing something unusual about the boy, had not granted him his release. After these two false starts, the boy found his real vocation on the printer's bench.

In 1825, when his apprenticeship expired, Garrison was twenty years old. Newburyport knew him as a promising young man, "a complete Baptist as to tenets," an ardent Federalist in his political opinions, and an expert compositor. What Newburyport did not know was that this promising young man was a born crusader and that he would give the world no rest until the evils he excoriated had been swept away. Nor did anyone yet realize that printer's ink, the only weapon Garrison used, was the most deadly in the world. Within three months of the end of his apprenticeship, he found himself the editor and publisher of his own paper. He did most of the writing, typesetting and printing, himself, but the public was not in sympathy with his Federalist leanings, and the dwindling circulation compelled him after less than a year to sell his paper to an editor more willing to cater to the truculently democratic tastes of the community. Discouraged by the prospect of earning his living in Newburyport, where there seemed to be no demand for independent thinking, Garrison set out for Boston. With no funds, and only one or two acquaintances among journeymen printers, he was always confident that if he lived long enough his name would be known to the world, "at least to such an extent that common enquiry shall be unnecessary."

The Boston that Garrison came to know, the Boston of Lyman Beecher and Channing and Bronson Alcott, was a pleasantly homogeneous city of thirty thousand inhabitants. Whether it was more moral than any other city in America, as Alcott maintained, it was certainly a city where men and women believed that all questions were moral questions, a city too where every kind of evil and injustice would soon be eradicated. One of the most obvious evils still to be overcome was drunkenness, and Garrison, with his father in mind, gravitated naturally to the editorship of the *National Philanthropist*, the first paper in the world devoted to "the suppression of intemperance and its kindred vices." Of all the dragons lurking in the path of mankind, drunkenness was the one Garrison was most eager to destroy. He even said once in an address to colored people: "God is my witness that, great as is my detestation of slavery and the foreign slave trade, I had rather be a slaveholder—yea, a kidnapper on the African coast—than sell this poison to my fellow-creatures for common consumption."

Later on in his career, when he was known as an abolitionist, some of his friends begged him to concentrate on slavery, and not to bore the world with his views on peace, theology, government, women's rights, temperance, and various other subjects on which he held strong opinions, but that was not his way. The words "expediency," "proportion" and "timeliness" meant nothing to him. Garrison's universe was componded of righteousness and sin. He believed that he alone was fortunate enough to be able to distinguish between the two, and a high sense of duty drove him to impose his convictions upon the rest of mankind.

II

In the second number of the *Philanthropist* appearing under his editorship, Garrison happened to comment on a law recently passed by the South Carolina legislature prohibiting the teaching of slaves to read and write. "There is," he declared, "something unspeakably pitiable and alarming in the state of that society where it is deemed necessary, for self-preservation, to seal up the mind and debase the intellect of man to brutal incapacity." There is nothing to indicate that the editor thought slavery a more serious evil than lotteries, imprisonment for debt, or the "desecration of the Sabbath" by the transportation of mails and of passengers on that day, but nevertheless the comment was prophetic of Garrison's future career.

His interest in the subject of slavery was soon confirmed by the arrival in Boston of a New Jersey Quaker, Benjamin Lundy, who may be regarded as the St. John the Baptist of the Abolition movement. Lundy was the first man in America to dedicate his life to the cause of the slave. As a young man he had gone to Wheeling, Virginia, to learn the harness-maker's trade, and there he had come in contact with slavery at its worst. Through Wheeling passed the "coffles" of slaves who were being transported by the newly built highway from Virginia to the Cotton States. Lundy watched the helpless Negroes stumbling along chained to each other, and the iron entered into his soul.

He became so obsessed by the horrors of slavery that he sold his business and devoted the proceeds to the organization of antislavery societies. In 1821, just after the admission of Missouri into the Union as a slave State, he launched an anti-slavery monthly, the *Genius of Universal Emancipation*. Lundy was a simple-hearted man who believed that the open discussion of slavery would bring about its downfall. The agitation over Missouri only proved to him that he must redouble his efforts. There was no printing shop in the little town of Mount Pleasant, Ohio, where he lived, which meant that he walked the twenty miles to Steubenville to get his newspaper printed, and returned with the entire edition on his back. That the *Genius* appeared so irregularly was due to the fact that Lundy made long journeys through the Southern States to gather experience and to preach his doctrines. In the eighteen-twenties it was still possible to talk dispassionately about slavery in the South. Lundy thought nothing of traveling hundreds of miles on foot or on horseback to any point where men were ready to consider forming an antislavery association. He carried type with him in his knapsack, and he was always ready to set up his paper wherever he happened to find himself, provided he could find a printer to run it off for him. Thanks largely to his efforts, the total number of antislavery associations had increased to nearly a hundred, representing every part of the Union except New England and the Cotton States.

By the time he arrived in Boston in the spring of 1828, Benjamin Lundy was recognized as the pioneer abolitionist in America. He lost no time in collecting as many clergymen of different sects as he could, and expounding his doctrine, "the gradual, though total, abolition of slavery in the United States." The meeting was not a success. Lundy was too much the gentle Quaker to be an effective speaker, and the holy men he gathered together were too timid to identify themselves with what threatened to be an unpopular cause. Garrison, who was present at the meeting, reported that he "might as well have urged the stones in the streets to cry out in behalf of the perishing captives. . . . One or two only were for bold and decisive action; but as they had neither station nor influence, and did not rank among the wise and prudent, their opinions did not weigh very heavily, and the project was abandoned. Poor Lundy! that meeting was a damper to his feelings; but he was not a man to be cast down, come what might."

However cast down he may have been, he had at least succeeded in kindling one flame that was to burn with ever-increasing intensity. Eleven years later, when Lundy died, Garrison acknowledged the debt. "I feel that I owe every-thing," he wrote, "instrumentally and under God, to Benjamin Lundy."

The relationship between the two men was not quite as unclouded as that generous tribute would suggest. As so often happens, the pupil outgrew his teacher or, to put it in Garrison's own words, "circumstances conspired to throw him somewhat in the shade, and to make me conspicuous in the eyes of the nation." Lundy had been so impressed with the fervor of Garrison's editorials that he persuaded him to move to Baltimore, where the *Genius of Universal Emancipation* was then being published. Together they would run the paper in a more businesslike way. They would publish it weekly instead of monthly, and the younger partner would be the resident editor, while Lundy traveled through the country canvassing for subscriptions.

Whatever other virtues Garrison may have possessed he was not a businessman. While Lundy was gathering in sub-scribers, Garrison, as he himself admitted, was knocking them off. From the very beginning they fought the great battle against slavery in different ways. Lundy hoped to win the South to his plans for the gradual abolition of slavery by the sheer reasonableness of his argument, nor did the fact that he was continually being threatened, and that he was once actually assaulted, by slave dealers on the streets of Baltimore, affect his unfailing good temper. To demand that the slave-holder should emancipate his slaves immediately, without compensation, was sheer folly. It would alienate those who were beginning to see the light, and it would harden the hearts of the slavery fanatics by showing that the alternative offered by the abolitionists was utterly impractical.

Garrison argued that since slavery was a monstrous evil it should be eradicated at once. His insistence on immediate emancipation was largely responsible for the dropping off of subscriptions and the dissolution of the partnership. He and Lundy had learned to respect each other's integrity, but they had also learned that they could not work together.

They differed also on the question of African colonization. Garrison was bitterly opposed to it. He regarded it as "wrong in principle and impotent in design." Lundy was ready to take advantage of any scheme that recognized the white man's obligations to the Negro. One of the reasons he had invited Garrison to become joint editor with him of the *Genius of Universal Emancipation* was that he himself wished to be free to make trips to Haiti, whenever necessary, with emancipated slaves. Colonization would always be a useful weapon in the great fight for freedom, and one not to be neglected merely because other weapons would be needed as well, before the battle was finally won. The idea of transporting the Negroes out of the country can be traced back to Jefferson's *Notes on Virginia*. "Among the Romans," as Jefferson pointed out, "emancipation required but one effort. The slave, when made free, might mix with, without staining the blood of his master. But with us a second is necessary, unknown to history. When

freed, he is to be removed beyond the reach of mixture."
Many of Jefferson's contemporaries, including Madison and
Monroe and Chief Justice Marshall, shared Jefferson's belief
that colonization in Africa, in Texas, in San Domingo or in
Haiti, offered the only feasible solution to slavery.

The Colonization Society grew out of a resolution passed
by the General Assembly of Virginia, December 23, 1816.
The purpose of the Society was to free the country of such
manumitted slaves as were prepared to go to Liberia. Under
the presidency of Washington's nephew, Judge Bushrod
Washington, and subsequently of Henry Clay, the Society
raised money to send agents to Africa to select a site for the
colony. Congress gave a fresh impetus to the movement in
1819 by passing an act providing that Negroes captured while
being illegally imported into the United States should be
returned to Africa, and appropriating a hundred thousand
dollars to be used by the Society for that purpose.

A threatened slave insurrection in Charleston, headed by a
free mulatto named Denmark Vesey, convinced several State
legislatures of the importance of the Colonization Society.
Vesey's desperate plan was so nearly successful that it left in
its wake an ineradicable distrust of free Negroes and a desire
to get them out of the country.

One of the main troubles of the Colonization Society was
that, generally speaking, the free Negroes did not want to be
transported to Liberia. In spite of the contempt with which
he was regarded, and the injustice with which he was treated,
the free Negro preferred America, the land he knew, to an
Africa thousands of miles away with which he felt he had
nothing in common. According to De Tocqueville, he even
preferred to live on in the South rather than migrate to the

North. Southern ways were at least familiar to him, and race prejudice seemed stronger in States that had got rid of slavery than in those which retained it. Certainly it is true that no one welcomed the free Negro and in many Northern States, including Illinois, Iowa, Indiana and Oregon, no free colored people were permitted to settle.

Jefferson's casual recommendation that America get rid of its Negroes was far more difficult to carry out than he had anticipated. In forty years of activity, from the first emigration in 1820 to the end of the year 1860, the Colonization Society succeeded in carrying over to Africa only 10,586 Negroes. A further thousand were sent out by State societies. Virginia, one of the States most anxious to send its free Negroes abroad, managed to get rid of only 700 in three and a half years of organized effort. How the remaining fifty-five thousand free Negroes were ever to be transported out of Virginia was a question no one cared to answer. Even supposing the Colonization Society had been enthusiastically supported by all those who wished the Negro well, it would have faced a gigantic task. At one moment, with the help of the merchant shipping fleets of western Europe, it might conceivably have transported the free Negroes out of America, but never the millions of slaves.

Garrison was unquestionably right in insisting that the Colonization Society could never grapple seriously with the problem of slavery. Its supporters liked to believe it was following a sensible middle-of-the-road policy. As one of them put it: "In the North, the ground of hostility is that we wage not war against slavery—in the South we are called an abolition society in disguise. . . . We would in a spirit of conciliation ask our brethren if the incompatibility of the views which they severally ascribe to the Society is not in itself a presumption that each may be gratuitous and that we have hit upon the golden mean between those conflicting opinions."

Garrison's attack upon this golden mean was thoroughly characteristic. He complained that the colonizers contented themselves with representing slavery as an evil, a misfortune, a calamity which had been entailed on them by former generations—and "not as an individual CRIME, embracing in its folds robbery, cruelty, oppression and piracy. They do not identify the criminals; they make no direct, pungent, earnest appeal to the conscience of men-stealers." After the failure of his partnership with Lundy, Garrison returned to Boston to spread the gospel of antislavery in New England. There he found "prejudice more stubborn, and apathy more frozen, than among slaveowners themselves." This time he would found his own paper, in which he would say exactly what he liked without diluting his opinions to suit others. The first issue of the *Liberator* appeared on January 1, 1831. Garrison had to rely on his friends to advance him the money for an office, for a printing press and for type. Even the paper on which the *Liberator* was printed was bought on credit. These same friends, though they agreed with Garrison's views, were not always in sympathy with his outspokenness. They would have preferred a less provocative name than the *Liberator*. One of them suggested as an alternative *The Safety Lamp*, but Garrison would have none of it. The name *Liberator* expressed exactly what he had in mind, and he refused to change it.

He was now twenty-five years old, full of confidence in his own abilities but still unknown except to a small group of would-be abolitionists who were beginning to realize that this sober young man meant every word he said, that he was utterly indifferent to public opinion, and that those who really believed that slavery was a monstrous evil would do well to rally round him.

Garrison had already proved his mettle by denouncing a shipowner of his native town of Newburyport, a certain Francis Todd, for engaging in the domestic slave trade. The fact that Todd was a highly respected citizen and that, in transporting seventy-five slaves from Baltimore to New Orleans, "chained in a narrow place between decks," he was doing nothing illegal, only infuriated Garrison the more. He wrote an article for the *Genius* excoriating Todd and his captain as "highway robbers and murderers." At the same time, he took advantage of a common enough incident to call attention to the amazing inconsistency of the government, which tolerated the domestic slave trade while treating the foreign traffic as piracy. To make sure that his shaft went home he sent a copy of his article to the Newburyport *Herald*, and another to Todd himself.

As he had hoped, Todd immediately sued him for defamation of character. In spite of the eloquent defense of an antislavery lawyer who volunteered his services gratis, it took the jury only fifteen minutes to bring in a verdict of guilty. The court imposed a fine of $50 and costs, amounting to $100 in all. This was a large sum at that period, probably more than Garrison had ever possessed at one time. Since he did not know anybody who could lend him the money, and since he certainly could not pay it himself, he was committed to prison.

No one ever entered the Baltimore city jail with a lighter heart. The warden treated him with unusual consideration and permitted him to wander about the prison at will, to receive as many visitors as he liked, and to write letters to the press. In the last issue of the *Genius*, he promised that his pen would never rest idle, and his voice never be suppressed, "while two million of my fellow-beings wear the shackles of slavery in my own guilty country." Among the friends to whom he wrote from the prison cell was the poet Whittier, who was planning to raise the money for his release when he was forestalled by a New York philanthropist. Arthur Tappan was one of those successful nineteenth century merchants who, as soon as he made money, began to reflect upon his obligations as a steward of the Lord. He supported a variety of causes including the movement for stricter Sabbath observance, the temperance crusade and the fight against tobacco. The abolition of slavery was merely one of the many reform movements that were close to his heart, but as soon as he heard of Garrison's trial and of his conviction he could not wait to pay the fine. Thanks to his generosity, Garrison was released on June 5, 1830, after an imprisonment of forty-nine days.

III

Garrison started the *Liberator* with few assets except his prison sentence. Other men before him had raised their voices against slavery, but no man before him had gone to jail for speaking out on the subject. From the newspaper point of view, he was a man to be reckoned with. His position was entirely different from that of the great army of philanthropists who deprecated slavery without knowing what to do about it. Garrison had no such doubts. He knew exactly

what should be done. All slaves should be liberated immediately without compensation to the owners. He did not consider it his duty as editor of the *Liberator* to prove that the
holding of slaves was criminal. He took it for granted that
slavery was a crime—a damning crime—and he set to work to
foment hatred of all those who battened on it or condoned it.

The *Liberator* played no favorites. If anything, Garrison
belabored the Northern apologists for slavery more vigorously
than he did the slave owners themselves. For those like Harrison Gray Otis, Boston's society mayor, who regarded
Southerners as "no more responsible for the existence of
slavery than for swamps, pine barrens, or any other physical
blemish of soil or local insalubrity," he felt the utmost contempt. Gradually he found himself involved in a struggle
against the organized religious sentiment, the political power,
the wealth and recognized respectability of the whole community. From having been brought up as a strict churchman,
he came to believe that the worst enemies of the Negro were
the professors of religion. Just as there is a school of writing
today that considers reticence in matters of sex synonymous
with hypocrisy, so Garrison considered any discussion of
slavery pusillanimous unless it were conducted in a tone of
righteous indignation. It was not enough to feel the pity of it,
as William E. Channing did. Channing, the most popular
Unitarian preacher in Boston, a man looked up to by all the
best people as the perfect blend of taste, scholarship and
wisdom, knew a good deal more about slavery than Garrison.
He had lived in the South as a young man and, though he
considered slavery a terrible evil, he was not ashamed to
number slave owners among his friends. He wrote a thoughtful essay on the subject, which Garrison reviewed in the

Liberator. Garrison summed up his objections under twenty-five heads, coming to the conclusion that the book was weak, contradictory and unsound. In other words, Channing was not an abolitionist, as Garrison understood the term. He did not lash out at sin.

The Rev. Lyman Beecher was another of Boston's famous clergymen who fought shy of the *Liberator.* Lyman Beecher was a more discreet abolitionist than his famous daughter. "Your zeal," he told Garrison, "is commendable, but you are mistaken. If you will give up your fanatical notions and be guided by us [the clergy], we will make you the Wilberforce of America." The idea of being guided by the clergy was the last thing that would have appealed to Garrison. He had weighed the clergy in the balance, and he had found them wanting.

The incendiary character of the *Liberator* was not fully developed until it had been running for several months. It appeared first as a modest, four-page weekly with a plain black letter heading surmounted by the motto, "Our Country is the World—Our Countrymen are Mankind." Garrison apparently had no idea that this formula was not original with him. Thomas Paine had already used it, having borrowed it from Socrates, but it was even more deeply true of Garrison. In the seventeenth number, the motto disappears and its place is taken by a crude engraving depicting a slave auction. On the right and in the immediate foreground, a placard surrounded by dejected Negroes and their prospective buyers announces "slaves, horses and other cattle to be sold at 12 o'c." In the background, a flag floats from the top of the Capitol, and just below it a whipping post is seen at which a slave is being flogged. As a piece of propaganda, the engraving could hardly have been bettered. Re-drawn and elaborated to meet the expansion of the paper, it remained at the masthead until slavery and the *Liberator* together disappeared from the stage of American history.

In spite of the mean surroundings in which it was born and the frugal habits of the editor, the *Liberator* was always in financial difficulties. The dingy office with ink-spattered walls which served Garrison as a combination home and workshop cost little enough to maintain, but a paper cannot live without subscribers, and these were hard to come by. Garrison had to rely mainly on the more intelligent colored people for his support. His bookkeeping was notoriously sketchy and by 1833, after two years of publication, the *Liberator* was running an annual deficit of $1,700. Obviously the 1,400 subscribers, of which only a quarter were white, could not of themselves keep the paper alive. At one moment Garrison seriously thought of giving it up, but negotiations with the New England Anti-Slavery Society "to get rid of the bookkeeping, money-getting part of the business" enabled him to keep his flag flying. The *Liberator* eventually became the official organ of the New England Society, which undertook to pay the editor two hundred dollars for a series of lectures. It was the first money Garrison had ever received for his abolitionist efforts.

Although the *Liberator* never paid expenses and never numbered more than three thousand subscribers, Garrison was not mistaken when he announced that, if he lived long enough, his name and his message would become known throughout the Union and across the seas. He did not foresee, though the irony of it must have struck him later, how much of his publicity he would owe to two Southern Governors of whom he had never heard. The *Liberator* had been running for almost a year when the Governor of Georgia and the Governor of Virginia wrote to Harrison Gray Otis, mayor of Boston, appealing to him to protect them against the circulation of abolitionist literature. They mentioned in particular "an incendiary newspaper published in Boston, and, as they alleged, thrown broadcast among their plantations, inciting to insurrection and its horrid results."

Mayor Otis had no idea what the governors were talking about. He had never seen a copy of the *Liberator*, nor had he or any member of the city government even heard of its existence. With some difficulty he procured a copy. "I am told," he said, "that it is supported chiefly by the free colored people; and that the number of subscribers in Baltimore and Washington exceeds that of those in this city, and that it is gratuitously left at one or two of the reading-rooms in this place. It is edited by an individual who formerly lived in Baltimore, where his feelings have been exasperated by some occurrences consequent to his publications there, on topics connected with the condition of slaves in this country." Otis was sure that this information would convince his friends in the South "of the insignificant countenance and support which the paper itself derives from this city."

Some years later, in an account of the same incident, he described how the city officers had ferreted out the paper and its editor. His office was "an obscure hole, his only visible auxiliary a Negro boy, and his supporters a very few insignificant persons of all colors. This information, with the consent of the aldermen, I communicated to the above-named governors, with the assurance of my belief that the new fanaticism had not made, nor was likely to make, proselytes among the respectable classes of our people. In this, however, I was mistaken."

Mayor Otis was indeed mistaken. At the same time that Garrison was stifling all projects of emancipation in the Border States by insisting that every slaveholder was a criminal, he was gathering around him in Boston a small but devoted band of followers, "such a fighting phalanx as the New England conscience had never before mustered." He had deliberately cut himself off from the great bulk of those who merely shook their heads over slavery and trusted that the Colonization Society would do something about it, by proclaiming that the whole colonization scheme was a fraud. He followed up this pronouncement by demanding that the public recognize immediate emancipation as the only honest remedy for the revolting disease of slavery. Garrison had been much encouraged by the British example in the West Indies. If it was possible for the British government to set free 800,000 Negroes by one stroke of the pen, why should Americans wring their hands and talk everlastingly about the hopelessness of their problem.

Early in 1833 Garrison received an announcement of a World Anti-Slavery Convention in London. The New England Anti-Slavery Society named him as its official delegate, and he was sent to England ostensibly to raise funds for a Negro school but actually to disabuse British emancipation leaders of the colonization heresy. Garrison's British mission was a complete success. According to John J. Chapman, "Colonization was a sort of obscene dragon that lay before the Palace of Slavery to devour or corrupt all assailants. Garrison attacked it like Perseus, with a ferocity which to this day is thrilling. His eyes, his words, and his sword flash and glitter. And he slew it. He cut off its supplies, he destroyed its reputation in Europe; and he thereby opened the path between the Abolition movement and the conscience of America." The colonization dream lingered on in the minds of some genuine friends of the Negro for many years, but Garrison's pamphlet and his speeches in England settled the question for all simon-pure abolitionists.

One of those who always clung to colonization as one of the several means of dealing with the Negro problem was Abraham Lincoln. As late at 1862 he invited a number of representative colored men to the White House, the first of their race ever so honored, and appealed to them to second his efforts to establish a colony in Central America. A group of land speculators had acquired a large tract of land, said to be rich in coal, on the Isthmus of Panama, for which they wanted laborers. Lincoln told the delegation frankly there was no place for them and their people in the United States. They would always suffer from discrimination. The response to the President's appeal was most unfavorable. After the interview, one of the Negroes wrote to Lincoln: "Pray tell us is our right to a home in this country less than your own?" The *Liberator* considered the proposal "puerile, impertinent and untimely."

IV

Garrison could now devote himself to the cause of immediate and unconditional emancipation. For this purpose he enlisted the services of an Englishman, George Thompson, who had played as great a part as Wilberforce himself in the emancipation of the British colonies. Thompson might have had a distinguished career in the House of Commons or at

the bar, but he sacrificed everything to carry on the battle for
Negro emancipation with Garrison in America. The two men
had taken to each other at first sight. They were the same
age, they had the same middle class background, the same
deeply religious training and the same aggressive temperament.
Garrison could not have picked a better man for his purpose.
The very fact that Thompson was an Englishman, and that
he undertook to lecture Americans on their duty to the Negro,
made him doubly effective.

If Garrison had a genius for irritating the respectable and
the well-to-do, Thompson irritated them still more, and that
was precisely what Garrison wanted. Only by agitation could
he hope to force the public to listen to him. The South had
given abolitionism a welcome publicity by associating Garrison's name with the Nat Turner uprising, and demanding that
the *Liberator* be suppressed. Just as that excitement was sub-
siding, the arrival of Thompson "startled the lethargic out of
their criminal sleep." The press raised the cry of foreign
interference. By what right did this foreigner dare offer an
opinion on American affairs! Garrison answered the outcry
he had been at such pains to arouse by pointing out that a
nation that had been helped into existence by Lafayette and
Kosciusko was hardly justified in complaining of foreign
interference. He would not have it that any American congressman could champion the rights of Hungarians, Irish,
Poles or any other people fighting for their liberty, while it
was impertinent for a foreigner to express his opinions about
slavery.

A crisis was reached in 1835 when it was announced that
George Thompson would be among the speakers at an anniversary meeting of the Boston Female Anti-Slavery Society.

Just previous to this meeting, fifteen hundred leading citizens had met together in Faneuil Hall and passed resolutions drafted by Harrison Gray Otis, in which the abolitionists were accused of wishing "to scatter among our Southern brethren firebrands, arrows and death," and of attempting to force acceptance of their views by inciting the slaves to revolt. One of the speakers prophesied that if the sentiments of the abolitionists prevailed, "it would be all over with the Union, which would give place to two hostile confederacies, with forts and standing armies." In other words the abolitionists, like their fellow fanatics in the South, were doing their best to precipitate a conflict.

After the Faneuil Hall demonstration, Mayor Theodore Lyman urged Garrison to discontinue his meetings until the public temper had cooled, assuring him, however, that the abolitionists would be protected in their rights if they insisted on exercising them. Garrison refused to interfere with the activities of the antislavery ladies, but the proprietor of the hall they had engaged changed his mind at the last moment and forbade them the use of the building.

The women refused to be thwarted. They engaged another hall and announced that they would hold their meeting on October 21, at three o'clock in the afternoon. As a grudging concession to public opinion, no speakers were announced and Thompson even left the city so that there should be no excuse for a disturbance. The mayor anticipated no trouble, but by the time Garrison reached the meeting he found a crowd of some two thousand people milling around the building, including "many gentlemen of property and influence." Garrison, like many self-made men, took a savage satisfaction in finding himself opposed by "gentlemen of property."

In spite of the noisy crowd outside, the meeting was called to order and the ladies began transacting their business. At this point Mayor Lyman appeared upon the scene and begged the ladies, in view of the menacing crowd, to leave the building. Accordingly they adjourned, very reluctantly, to meet at the house of one of their members a few blocks away. Even then the crowd was not satisfied. Thompson was not there, the ladies were not there, but Garrison, the original trouble-maker, was there, and they would not disperse until he had left the building. Lyman suggested that he should leave by a rear window to avoid further trouble. In Garrison's own account of the matter, three or four of the rioters started to throw him out of the window and then changed their minds. "So they drew me back, and coiled a rope about my body— probably to drag me through the streets. I bowed to the mob, and requesting them to wait patiently until I could descend, went down upon a ladder that was raised for that purpose. I fortunately extricated myself from the rope, and was seized by two or three powerful men, to whose firmness, policy, and muscular energy I am probably indebted for my preservation." By these men, presumably Lyman's constables, Garrison was escorted to the city jail where he was lodged for the night as a disturber of the peace. On the following morning he was discharged.

The detailed account of this episode, to which Garrison's sons devote more than a hundred pages in the official *Life* of their father, shows that Garrison himself behaved with dignity, courage and common sense. The assumption, readily accepted by his biographers, that everyone opposed to him was a scoundrel is not so easy to accept. Though there may have been a few Southerners among them, there is no reason to suppose that the 1,500 citizens who attended the Faneuil Hall meeting were not just as high-minded and just as courageous as Garrison himself. They were disgusted with his tactics, as were many of the abolitionists in other parts of the country, but there is nothing to prove they were responsible for the mob. Probably they regretted the free publicity he received at their hands. It would have suited them far better if he had remained unknown.

Garrison was always too ready to believe that those who were not with him were against him. Mayor Lyman, for instance, as a public-spirited Bostonian devoted to good works of all kinds, probably sympathized with Garrison's aims while disapproving of his demagoguery. He may not have been a hero, but he managed to keep the peace and to extricate Garrison from the hands of an angry mob, for which he hardly deserved to be vilified. Garrison complained that his trousers were torn during the fracas, and that he lost his hat, but surely these indignities were a small price to pay for the martyr's halo. This was the second time he had gone to jail, not just for expressing abolitionist sentiments, but for defending the right of free speech. That was the way for an agitator to get his name before the public, and no one was more aware of it than Garrison.

The extent of the publicity Garrison and Thompson had won for their cause can hardly be overestimated. When Thompson went back to England in 1836, he left behind him 328 antislavery societies, many of them called into being, and others revitalized, by his eloquence. In his *Rise and Fall of the Confederacy*, Jefferson Davis notes that up until 1835 the abolitionists could hardly be considered a power for evil since they were just as unpopular in the North as in the South. He dates the turn in the tide from that year. "Chief among them," says Davis, "was an Englishman, one Thompson, whose mission was to prepare the way for the dissolution of the Union." How such a man could have been so successful in overcoming the opposition to him, Davis could never understand.

Among those who could have corroborated Jefferson Davis' opinion of the abolitionists was a young Boston lawyer, Wendell Phillips, who was to become the greatest antislavery orator of them all, but who in 1835 was still uncommitted to the cause. Phillips represented all that was most patrician in Boston society. He was the kind of young man for whom, when he was an undergraduate at Harvard, the family carriage would be sent out to Cambridge every Saturday morning to bring him home for the weekend. He was also the kind of young man who flared up at the sight of cruelty or injustice. *Noblesse oblige* was no mere catchword to Wendell Phillips.

One afternoon, just after he had set up his law office in Boston, he was distracted from his lawbooks by a commotion in the street below him. Some unfortunate creature was being dragged along the street, with a rope around his waist, by an angry-looking crowd. The victim, it appeared, was a troublesome newspaperman named Garrison. Phillips was infuriated and at the same time puzzled. He was puzzled because the crowd seemed to be made up of respectable-looking citizens instead of the usual hoodlums, and he was infuriated because nobody seemed to be doing anything to protect the victim. Why did not the Mayor call out the militia? "You fool!" exclaimed one of the bystanders in answer to his question. "Don't you see that the militia is in front of you?" From that moment Wendell Phillips began to drift away from his Beacon Street associates and to identify himself more and more with the abolitionists. It disgusted the provincial patriot in him that Boston, the cradle of civil liberty in America, should deny Garrison or anybody else the right of free speech.

Phillips was not originally drawn to the cause of emancipation by his compassion for the Negro—that was to come later—but rather by his jealous regard for the rights of the white man. If free speech had to be stifled in order that slavery should survive, then slavery must be an evil thing. The unspeakable evil of it was soon brought home to him. The spectacle of Garrison being dragged through the streets might possibly have faded from his mind, but the murder of Elijah Lovejoy by a proslavery mob in Alton, Illinois, was something no civilized man could or should forget.

The Rev. Elijah Parish Lovejoy, editor of the Alton *Observer*, was a mild-mannered, fearless man who wanted to live at peace with his neighbors, but who would speak his mind about slavery. That was his only offense. A proslavery mob broke up his presses and threw them into the Mississippi River. Lovejoy refused to be intimidated. Each time his press was destroyed he bought another. This happened three times. Finally he was shot and killed while, with the aid of a handful of friends, he was trying to defend his fourth press from the fury of the mob. The news of Lovejoy's murder reached Boston on November 19, 1837, twelve days after the event. A committee of one hundred distinguished citizens, headed by William Ellery Channing, immediately called a meeting in Faneuil Hall. Garrison wisely abstained from any official connection with the meeting. He realized that he himself was an unpopular figure and he did not want to confuse the issue. The aldermen were at first reluctant to permit the use of a municipally owned building for what promised to be a highly controversial meeting, but the feeling against them ran so high that they changed their minds and granted the petitioners the use of the hall "in the daytime, lest if it should be held in the evening Boston might see another mob."

Faneuil Hall has always been identified by good Bostonians with the cause of liberty. It was presented to the municipality in 1742 by Peter Faneuil, the son of a Huguenot refugee who had been driven out of France by the revocation of the Edict of Nantes. He could think of no better way of commemorating the injustice that had been done to his father than to donate to the city in the new world, where he had settled and prospered, a hall to be used freely by the people for the discussion of public affairs. In the revolutionary days, Sam Adams and John Hancock had held meetings in that hall to protest against the stamp tax and the tax on tea. It was all the more remarkable therefore when at this meeting, called to protest against Lovejoy's murder as a crime against the statutory right of free speech, the Attorney-General of the State, one William Austin, rose to defend the slayers of Lovejoy by comparing them to the men who organized the Boston Tea Party, "Lovejoy," he concluded, "had died as the fool dieth."

Wendell Phillips could not allow that speech to go unchallenged. He pushed his way to the platform and denounced Austin in one of the greatest speeches that ever echoed through Faneuil Hall. When "the whirlwind applause had died away" and the question of the guilt of the murderers was put to a vote, the whole hall resounded with the roar of "Aye!" Not a single voice was raised in their defense. The murder of Lovejoy and still more the amazing attempt to defend the murderers, in Faneuil Hall of all places, marks a crisis in the abolitionist movement. For one thing, it revealed the eloquence and fixed the destiny of Wendell Phillips. From now on he became more relentless in his castigation of slavery, more bitter in his abuse of slave owners, than Garrison himself. No longer could Harrison Gray Otis, or anybody else, dismiss the abolitionists as mere cranks. They were becoming respectable. Through the stupidity of their enemies they were now able to identify their cause with freedom of speech and freedom of the press. The American people, like the wedding guest in *The Ancient Mariner*, could not choose but hear.

V

Garrison's biographers would have us believe that the whole abolition movement in America stemmed from him and from the devoted band of followers he gathered around him, but Garrison was too much of an eccentric, too much a law unto himself, ever to become the national antislavery leader he would have liked to be. There were many other workers in the vineyard, in the Border States, in New York and in Ohio, who went their own way without paying any attention to what was happening in New England. If they thought of Garrison at all, it was only to dismiss him as a crank who befogged the issue by combining antislavery with a number of other unrelated reforms.

Garrison was particularly interested in the question of women's rights and, since women were fully as competent as men in arousing the conscience of the nation to the evils of slavery, he demanded that women should serve with men on the committees of the National Anti-Slavery Society. The question came to a head at the convention held in New York in 1840. Garrison's opponents claimed that putting a woman on a committee with men was "contrary to the usages of civilized society," but by chartering a boat in Boston and filling it with his supporters Garrison arrived in New York with the votes necessary to control the convention. "It was our antislavery boatload," he explained later, "that saved our society from falling into the hands of the new organizers, or rather disorganizers." Garrison's victory resulted in a serious split in the abolitionist ranks.

Of all his idosyncrasies, the one that was most alarming to his fellow abolitionists in other parts of the country was his repudiation of the Constitution, and indeed of the whole machinery of government. Slavery, according to Garrison, could be destroyed only by moral suasion. It was useless to try to fight it by political means. He honestly believed that "the governments of this world, whatever their titles or forms . . . are all Anti-Christ; that they can never, by human wisdom, be brought into conformity with the will of God." On these grounds, he could not believe in the sacredness of the compact formed between the free and the slave states. He did not even believe in going to the polls, since every government relies on force and force is inherently evil. The more Garrison pondered over the state of the nation, the more convinced he was that law-abiding abolitionists were in an impossible dilemma. Slave owners could always take refuge, when hard-pressed, behind constitutional guarantees. That was exactly the position taken by Calhoun. The Constitution was the bulwark of slavery. Garrison, therefore, was being perfectly consistent when, on July 4, 1854, in protest against the Fugitive Slave Law, he burnt a copy of the Constitution, "the source and parent of all other atrocities—a covenant with Death and an agreement with Hell."

It was natural enough that the Southern fire-eaters should have felt a sneaking respect for such fanaticism. Senator Howell Cobb of Georgia did not hesitate to admit that Garrison was "bolder and honester" than the Republicans. Certainly he was a lunatic, judged by Cobb's standards, but at least he was consistent, as lunatics often are. He refused to attack slavery and defend the Constitution at the same time. The more he thought about slavery and emancipation the more convinced he was that the position of slavery within the framework of the Constitution was impregnable. One could not be destroyed without the other.

A few abolitionists may have followed Garrison in rejecting government, but the growing army of those who were opposed to slavery, including James G. Birney, the antislavery leader of Kentucky, believed that if slavery were ever to be overthrown it would be by political means. As a practical man, he had no patience with Garrison's philosophic anarchism. Such abolitionists, he thought, "were brambles without fruit; a million of them would effect nothing. They fought like a Chinese army, rattling tin pans to frighten the enemy."

Birney was a slaveholder by inheritance, one of those ardently sincere men who, having seen slavery at its best as well as its worst, had liberated his own slaves and provided generously for their future. In attacking slavery in Kentucky, he was for a long time the only abolitionist who was grappling with slavery in a slave State. He did not believe in colonization, though he had supported it at one time as a necessary step in the evolution of antislavery opinion. Nor did he believe in gradual emancipation, any more than Garrison. Birney moved more slowly than Garrison but more surely. Since slavery had died a natural death in the Middle and Eastern States, he assumed that it was in the process of extinction in the South as well. It was only when he came up against the terrible inertia of slave owners in his own State of Kentucky, and when he realized that freedmen could not be employed as laborers by the side of slaves, that he came to the conclusion that gradual emancipation was not feasible. Though his prejudices were all against it, he decided very reluctantly that immediate emancipation was the only way.

If Birney had not been struck down by paralysis in 1845, at the very height of his powers, it is at least conceivable that the tragedy of war might have been avoided. He was the one abolitionist whom the South listened to with respect. His correspondence with Franklin Elmore, a Congressman from South Carolina and an intimate friend of Calhoun, proves that the slave owners, if approached in the right spirit, were not hopelessly deaf to argument. In 1838, Birney had sent an antislavery publication to Calhoun, together with a note stating that it was sent to him because he appeared more interested than other Southern politicians in getting accurate information about antislavery activities. Such letters did not usually meet with a friendly response from Southerners, but this one was answered by Elmore, as representing the slave power in Congress, without a trace of bad temper.

Elmore wrote to Birney as a "man of intelligence, sincerity and truth," for further information about the attitude of the abolitionists to the Constitution. He knew from Birney's "well-established character and fairness" that he "would make no statements of facts which were not known or believed by you to be true." Birney replied in the same vein. He assured Elmore that the abolitionists regarded the Constitution with "unabated affection." They had nothing to ask except what the Constitution authorized. The contrast between these sentiments and the motto of the *Liberator*, "The Federal Constitution—a covenant with Death and agreement with Hell," shows how far the main body of abolitionists had separated themselves from the lunatic fringe of Garrisonians.

Birney cleared the abolitionist cause of cranks, and by so doing he made it appeal to the great section of the Northwest that Garrison never reached. Through Birney abolitionism forced its way into politics. Everywhere, except in New England, one local society after another passed resolutions declaring the exercise of the voting right to be a sacred duty. The question was not whether an abolitionist should vote or not, but whether he should vote for anyone who had not yet committed himself to the antislavery cause. Most leaders of the movement thought he should not, but until an antislavery political party took the field there was no way for abolitionist sentiment to make itself felt.

After many false starts, a National Third Party Anti-Slavery Convention was called to meet at Albany, on April 1, 1840, at which Birney was selected as the presidential candidate. The new party, generally known as the Liberty party, had at first no name and it adopted no platform. With William Henry Harrison, the hero of Tippecanoe, running as the candidate of the Whig party, not many abolitionists, most of whom were Whigs, could be expected to forsake the bandwagon in favor of a candidate who could not possibly win. Birney polled only 7,000 votes, but abolitionism had at least got its toe in the door. In 1844 he was again nominated for

President, and this time the abolitionists played a significant part in determining the outcome. Thanks to the 62,000 votes Birney diverted away from Henry Clay, the election was won by James K. Polk, the first of the presidential "dark horses." Clay had followed Calhoun in accusing the abolitionists of carrying on an agitation which, unless stopped, would break up the Union. In spite of his unsatisfactory record on slavery, his wobbling on the annexation of Texas, Clay was very nearly successful, but in the pivotal State of New York there were just enough abolitionist votes to defeat him.

During the twenty years that elapsed between Birney's first campaign and the election of Lincoln, the trickle of 7,000 votes cast for the Liberal party had swollen into the torrent that swept Lincoln into the White House. The Liberal party, well organized and hopeful, evolved into the Free Soil, and finally into the Republican, party. Birney had always insisted that one good Congressman could do more for the cause than a hundred lecturers, and the election of 1860, though he did not live to see it, proved that he was right. In spite of all his efforts there was always a great army of abolitionists who either fought shy of politics altogether, or could not bring themselves to break away from their regular party allegiances. Garrison and Phillips would not besmirch themselves with politics at all. There were many others who without going as far as the two antislavery champions were generally cynical about politics. They felt that too often politicians had used the slavery issue to promote their own selfish aims.

Among those who went their own way oblivious of the Eastern abolitionists was Theodore Weld, one of the most modest and at the same time most effective of all the nineteenth century crusaders for freedom. Weld could never have thrown in his lot with the Garrisonians on account of their extraneous projects, nor could he join any political group such as Birney's Liberal party since no politician would affirm the rights of women, the one extraneous project about which he felt very strongly. He made his greatest contribution to the antislavery cause by training young men and women and sending them out to convert others. Himself "eloquent as an angel and powerful as thunder," he abolitionized vast areas in Pennsylvania, Ohio, and western New York, that would never have been reached by anybody else. Weld also wrote a book, *Slavery as It Is*, constructed out of materials the South itself had furnished. From the files of Southern papers he culled scores of instances of floggings, brandings, and shootings, to prove that slavery and brutality were inseparable. Harriet Beecher Stowe quarried the incidents for her own enormously effective best-seller from Weld's grim pile of iniquity. *Uncle Tom's Cabin* reached millions of readers, whereas Weld's cumbersome tract was read only by the converted. It would perhaps have been more accurate to call it *The Evils of Slavery* but, like all abolitionists, Weld refused to admit there could be any redeeming features in an institution that was so inherently vicious.

In every other respect, except their conviction that slavery was vile and slave owners brutal, the abolitionists differed so much among themselves that it was never possible for them to unite.

"The family feuds of the abolitionists were a stench in the nostrils of the nation," as Garrison's friend Lewis Tappan once remarked, and Weld agreed with him. As time went on, the root and branch abolitionists were almost as opposed to the free-soilers as they were to slavery itself. Lincoln's theory that slavery would eventually disappear, provided it was prevented from spreading, was anathema to them. They could not even agree on the slogan "immediate emancipation." Some insisted the words must be taken literally, others construed it to mean "immediate emancipation, gradually accomplished."

Whether or not the fire-eaters in the South knew of these squabbles in the ranks of their opponents, they always identified Garrison with the abolitionist cause, and they whipped up sentiment for secession by proclaiming far and wide that the hatred of slave owners expressed by Garrison, Thompson and Wendell Phillips was characteristic of all abolitionists. Garrison might deny any specific connection with the Nat Turner uprising, but he could not deny that the *Liberator* wished the slaves success in their insurrections. When Wendell Phillips spoke of the South as "one great brothel, where half a million women are flogged to prostitution," Southerners in general accepted the statement as a fair expression of Northern opinion. Thanks to the fanatics on both sides of the Mason-Dixon line the leaven of hatred was always working. Actually, George Thompson did not say that Southern slaves ought to cut the throats of their masters, nor could anyone have named the city in the South that was said to have offered three thousand dollars for Lewis Tappan's ears—Tappan was president of the New York Abolition Society—but such rumors were eagerly believed. Rumors would never have sufficed to drive a fundamentally fair-minded people to war, if there had not been definite acts as well to lend substance to the threats and angry speeches of the disunionists. The murder of Elijah Lovejoy made far more converts to abolitionism than Garrison's editorials in the *Liberator*, and the attack on Charles Sumner in the Senate, John Brown's massacre of innocent men in Kansas, and the raid on Harper's Ferry all contributed to the growing feeling, originally confined to the extremists, that the time had come for the two sections of the country to separate.

VI

Of all the earnest, high-minded men and women who helped to drive a wedge between the North and the South during the years between the Mexican and the Civil War no one was more bent on forcing the issue than the famous senator from Massachusetts, Charles Sumner. No Garrisonian declaiming against the Constitution, no fervent disciple of John C. Calhoun, ever led the way more deliberately to the point of no return. Not that Sumner was at all indifferent to the horrors of war. While still a comparatively unknown young lawyer he had made a name for himself in Boston as an advocate of pacifism. In the first important speech of his life, a patriotic address delivered in Tremont Temple on July 4, 1845, he had astounded his audience, accustomed to a conventional recital of the stirring deeds of the Revolution, by denouncing in scathing terms the misguided patriotism which glorified deeds of war. Sumner drove his point home by comparing the cost to the nation of the *Ohio*, a ship-of-the-line then lying in Boston Harbor, with the annual expenditure of Harvard College. The warship, he concluded, cost as much to build and to maintain as a college. Each porthole was the financial equivalent of one professor.

It was not a tactful speech considering that the officers of the *Ohio* had been specially invited to grace the occasion, but then Charles Sumner was not a tactful man. His lack of tact was as notorious as his lack of humor or his unconscious arrogance. At the same time he possessed certain positive qualities which society has always respected. He was well educated, he was as upright as a flagpole, and he was forever ready and eager to tilt at any form of injustice. The greater the odds against him, the more he reveled in the fight. Unlike most of the political figures of his generation, he was very much at home in Europe. Sometimes he wearied his friends at home by telling them of all the distinguished people he had met abroad in the course of his travels and yet, beneath the European veneer, there was a moral fervor about Sumner, a "sacred animosity" against evil, to quote his own words, that stamped him unmistakably as a New Englander.

By the middle of the century, the shadow of slavery loomed so large over the nation that the various reform movements in which he was interested were crowded out of his mind. In 1849, as chairman of the Peace Committee of the United States, he had issued an address recommending that an American delegation attend the Second General Peace Congress to be held at Frankfort. Representatives of the leading nations of Europe were to present plans for the revision of international law and for the establishment of a World Court. Sumner, who was known as one who believed that war was an outdated method of settling disputes, was chosen as one of the delegates to the Congress, but at the last moment he declined. Perhaps he was dimly aware that there were some issues very much at stake in his own country that did not lend themselves to negotiation. He would undoubtedly have repudiated the charge of inconsistency, but there is something ironic in the fact that the champion of arbitration in 1850 stood out resolutely against sending any delegates from Massachusetts to the

Peace Convention held in Washington on the eve of the war. In his last frantic search for a compromise, Senator Crittenden found no one more stubborn, more determined not to yield an inch, than Senator Sumner.

Many things at home had combined to change his opinion about the efficacy of arbitration. The annexation of Texas, the Mexican War, and most of all the Fugitive Slave Act, had created a cleavage in many a Northern household, particularly in Massachusetts, between those who were willing to compromise in order to settle a troublesome issue once and for all, and those like Sumner who insisted that concessions would settle nothing. "Nothing," said Sumner, "can be settled which is not right. Nothing can be settled which is against freedom. Nothing can be settled which is against divine law."

Most of the people in Boston who "counted," the men of property and refinement, the substantial merchant families on State Street whose fortunes were tied up with cotton—"lords of the loom," as Wendell Phillips called them—sided with Daniel Webster in his willingness to swallow the Fugitive Slave Act. The task of hounding a few runaways and returning them to slavery, distasteful though it was, was infinitely less distasteful than the alienation of one's Southern clients, the disruption of business and the prospect of civil war. Reasonable men, they argued, should be content to follow the lead of such great-hearted patriots as Webster and Henry Clay. As events proved, reasonable men did follow them. After months of wrangling, the Great Compromise of 1850 became law. "I can now sleep at nights," wrote Daniel Webster, "the Union stands firm."

Unfortunately for those who congratulated themselves on having resolved all their differences with the Southern States, there was always an intensely vocal minority of unreasonable men who could never make peace with slavery. In the factories of the mill towns, in the rural printing shops, and on the lonely farms, the rumbling protests inspired by Garrison could not be stilled. Many of Garrison's readers, Sumner among them, did not agree with him that the Constitution was "a covenant with death" and should therefore be annulled, but they were grateful to him for his weekly invective against compromise.

A few patricians like Wendell Phillips prided themselves on holding fast to the prejudices that Webster begged them to conquer. Phillips and Sumner traveled by different routes toward the same goal. As a professional agitator, Phillips never appreciated the role that a political party might play in furthering the cause of emancipation. Sumner, a political animal if there ever was one, felt that the battle against slavery could be waged effectively only in Washington.

Sumner was elected to the Senate in 1851, much to the disgust of his conservative friends, by a well-managed coalition of Democrats and Conscience Whigs. The followers of Webster regarded him as a traitor to his class and snubbed him accordingly, but whatever Boston society might think of him a far wider audience acclaimed him as their champion. One greeting in particular he took to heart and never forgot. "You told me once," wrote Theodore Parker, one of the most ardent of Garrison's supporters, "that you were in morals, not in politics. Now I hope you will show you are still in morals, although in politics. I hope you will be the Senator with a conscience."

That hope was certainly gratified. From the moment he took his seat in the Senate, Sumner's conscience was always on parade. However complicated the problem, and slavery was the most complicated problem the nation had ever faced, Sumner's conscience could always be relied upon to provide a ready answer. It was as simple for him to settle the question as it was for the Southern fire-eaters, and curiously enough his answer was the same as theirs—follow the Constitution. But, according to Sumner, the Constitution did not sanction slavery, and since slavery was a monstrous evil it should be terminated at once. Freedom was national whereas slavery was only sectional. In the official view of the South, which incidentally corresponded with that of the Garrisonians, the founding fathers had expressly guaranteed slavery along with other forms of personal property. Far from being a national evil, it was a national benefit, to the Negro as much as to the white man.

Starting from their respective hypotheses, Sumner and the fanatics in the South launched a campaign of reciprocal vilification which spread to the press of both sections and gradually involved the whole nation. Sumner seized upon the controversy over Kansas, whether the Territory was to come into the Union as a free or as a slave State, to pronounce what he called "the most thoroughgoing philippic ever uttered in a legislative body." It was an elaborate speech and it took five hours to deliver. For those who expected an accurate presentation of the facts about Kansas it was a disappointment, but Sumner's conscience was never concerned with facts unless the facts bore on the depravity of slaveholders. Nor was his audience in any mood to listen to a dispassionate analysis of fraudulent elections, which was what the situation demanded. Sumner's conscience directed him to pour oil on the fire rather than water. He began by assuming the truth of every charge made against the slave power in Kansas, and ignoring all the evidence on the other side. Major John Sedgwick, who was stationed in Kansas at the time and who eight years later as Major General John Sedgwick gave his life for the Union, thought that most of the atrocities had been committed by the Free Soil party, but any such evidence, even if it had come his way, Sumner would have brushed aside as the ravings of a lunatic. He had prepared his speech with infinite pains, committed it to memory, practiced it before the glass, and nothing would induce him to alter it.

The crime against Kansas was nothing less than "the rape of virgin territory compelling it to the hateful embrace of slavery." The criminal (slave power) has "an audacity beyond that of Verres, a subtlety beyond that of Machiavelli, a meanness beyond that of Bacon, and an ability beyond that of Hastings." The long string of erudite insults reached their climax in an attack upon the much beloved Senator Butler of South Carolina who, said Sumner, "has chosen a mistress to whom he has made his vows and who, although ugly to others, is always lovely to him; although polluted in the sight of the world, is chaste in his sight—I mean the harlot, Slavery."

That Sumner honestly thought he was serving the cause of freedom by such language is hard to believe. Fashions change in rhetoric as in everything else, but even so the Senate was disgusted. Senator Cass of Michigan, a devoted Union man and not a slaveholder, delivered the official rebuke: "Such a speech—the most un-American and unpatriotic that ever grated on the ears of the members of this high body—I hope never to hear again here or elsewhere." For a moment Sumner was under a cloud, but only for a moment. While Senators were shaking their heads over his extraordinary performance, Sumner was suddenly transfigured into a national hero, a martyr for freedom. The man responsible for this amazing transformation was a Southerner, Congressman Preston S. Brooks of South Carolina, a nephew and a devoted admirer of Senator Butler. In an evil hour for the South, Brooks made up his mind that the only suitable answer to Sumner was severe corporal punishment. Accordingly, while Sumner was sitting at his desk after the Senate had adjourned, Brooks strode up to him and, without giving him a chance to defend himself, struck him over the head with a gutta-percha cane. How severely Sumner was injured has always been a matter of dispute, but by the time Brooks had finished his chastisement Sumner was lying on the floor unconscious.

Southerners accused Sumner of shamming. The doctor who first attended him took four stitches in his scalp and declared him ready to return to duty after a few days of rest, but the promise that he would be able to take up his work again was not fulfilled for a long time. Probably the nervous state he was in at the time intensified the effect of his injuries. He himself complained of perpetual headache and nervous prostration, but Southerners pointed out that during the trip to Europe to recover his health he indulged in a continuous round of social entertainments that might well have reduced any traveler to a state of exhaustion. Whatever the effect upon his health may have been, he played no part in political life for the next three years, during which his empty seat in the Senate won him more friends than any speech he ever made. There it stood, a silent but eloquent reminder of Southern "chivalry." Of all the varied instruments that goaded a reluctant people to war nothing, not even Harriet Beecher Stowe's pen, or the rope around John Brown's neck, was more effective than "Bully" Brooks's gutta-percha cane.

The tidal wave of indignation that swept over the North following the assault on Sumner, swamped the handful of critics who remembered and regretted the tone of his speeches. In the South, feeling about the Brooks-Sumner affair was not nearly as clear-cut as in the North. South Carolina, as was to be expected, approved. Any one who spoke of a South Carolina Senator in the disgusting way Sumner had spoken deserved to be chastised, but in the other Southern States opinion was more temperate. No one wasted any sympathy on Sumner himself, but many felt his punishment should not have been inflicted in the Senate. Planters and businessmen who had any connections with the North realized that, no matter how many gold-headed canes Charleston might send him, Brooks had done their cause incalculable harm. Once again the cause of free speech had become identified with abolitionism.

Sumner in the meantime was touring France and England in search of health. Wherever he went he was hailed as a martyr in a great cause. Europe had learned of the brutality of slave owners from *Uncle Tom's Cabin* and here was Sumner, a living rebuke to the sceptics who could not believe that things were as bad as Mrs. Stowe had painted them. After an absence of three and a half years, he felt well enough to take up his duties again in the Senate. He might have gone a long way toward healing the rift if, in his first speech after his long illness, he had held out the hand of friendship to the South, but that was not Sumner's way. Unaware that slavery was no longer an issue in Kansas, he took up the issue again on June 4, 1860, exactly where he had left it on May 20, 1856. In another grand assault on slavery, described by a Western editor as "able, exasperating and useless," he showed he could be just as offensive as ever. Whatever sickness had done to him, it had not dulled his powers of invective. At a time when other Republicans were doing their utmost to reassure the South, when Seward was trying to make men forget his remarks about an "irrepressible conflict," Sumner was still harping on his favorite theme that no man could own a slave without becoming a barbarian and a brute. The bewildered Southerner who still clung to the Union may have been forgiven for wondering whether the Republican party was holding out an olive branch or a naked sword.

All through the winter of 1860 and the early spring of 1861, Sumner was haunted by the fear that the Republican party would make some disgraceful compromise. While Lincoln was watching and waiting, and while Seward and Charles Francis Adams were searching for some formula, some way of conciliating the Border States without conceding too much, Sumner, wrapped in the toga of rectitude, was exhorting his countrymen not to surrender "those impregnable principles of human rights which constitute our Northern forts." The idea of clothing a firm policy in conciliatory language had never occurred to him. His mind did not work that way. Brooks's assault had convinced him that the whole slave-owning class was made up of whisky-drinking ruffians. With such men one did not parley. And yet, though he refused to listen to any of the last-minute compromises, Sumner was not one of those who looked forward, like some of the other radical Republicans in the Senate, to a little bloodletting.

There was still another way out, the way of Garrison and Phillips. Cut the Southern States adrift. Let them go, to be devoured as they surely would be, by anarchy and slave insurrections. A great, free Northern republic, including possibly

Canada, offered a more tempting prospect than the old Union painfully reconstructed by war or by compromise. Sumner was too ambitious a politician to commit himself entirely to the abolitionists, but he was closer to them in many ways than to the average orthodox Republican.

During the war, and still more during the Reconstruction, Sumner posed as one of those who had never faltered in his devotion to the Union. Though he was a no-compromise man as far as slavery was concerned, he was not always opposed to secession. In a letter to Governor Andrew of Massachusetts, written on January 8, 1861, a letter which he carefully omitted from his published correspondence, he shows distinct signs of weakening on the crucial issue of the Union: "If possible we must avoid civil war; indeed to avert this dread calamity I will give up, if necessary, territory and State; but I will not give up our principles."

Always with Sumner we come back to the question of principles. Whenever they were involved he never wavered. Like all fanatics he was a one-idea man. The essential virtue was firmness, by which he meant a refusal to admit that there might be more than one side to a question. Just as the fire-eaters could not understand that Northerners were more and more coming to look upon slavery as a moral issue, so to men like Sumner it was incomprehensible that Southerners in general, whether they were slave owners or not, looked on slave labor as a matter of economics. We know now that the fanatics on both sides were only half right, that slavery was an immensely complicated problem bound up with morality, politics, society and economics, and that anyone who tried to approach it as Sumner did was bound to make a mess of it.

VII

Of all those in the North who saw the question quite simply as a matter of right and wrong, no one was more fatally consistent than John Brown. He realized, as Garrison, Phillips, Birney and Sumner never did, that immediate emancipation could never be effected by moral suasion or by the ballot box. These men and many others expended their energies in writing, talking and organizing antislavery societies to provide more talkers and more writers. They thought to destroy slavery by arraigning it on a lecture platform or on the floor of the Senate. By the end of the century slavery would have died a natural death, with or without their efforts, but John Brown was one of those who would not wait. While others talked and wrote, he killed and died.

Wendell Phillips once acclaimed John Brown as "a Lord High Admiral of the Almighty with his commission to sink every pirate (i.e., slaveholder) he meets on God's ocean." Whether we think of him as a divinely commissioned pirate, a Puritan, a Hebrew prophet or a Scotch covenanter, as his friends variously called him, or as just a maniac, as his enemies have always asserted, John Brown was certainly not a leader of anything that could be called a movement. He was one of those fanatics, occasionally thrown up by history, who assume to themselves a role of criminal violence in order to achieve their ends. Slavery was such a monstrous evil in his eyes that he was ready and willing to commit any crime, including murder, in order to get rid of it. He had already made a name for himself as a Negro raider and even as a killer long before he conceived his ambitious plan of starting a slave stampede for freedom at Harper's Ferry.

The John Brown legend of a noble soul battling against injustice and oppression has had to be put together out of the most unpromising materials. Up to the moment of his capture in the engine house of Harper's Ferry, there was nothing about the man himself or about his career that could possibly be construed as either likeable or admirable. An uncompromising Puritan with all the instincts of a patriarchal despot, he had shown himself quite incapable of providing a decent living for his large family. His first wife died insane after bearing him seven children. The taint of insanity hovered over both sides of the Brown family. Within less than a year he was married again, to a competent, stoical woman who in the course of twenty-one years produced another thirteen children. Several of them died in infancy; but with the large brood that survived, and with his uncomplaining wife, he shifted from place to place, from Ohio to Pennsylvania, to Massachusetts and New York, dabbling in one business after another, always hoping to make his fortune out of some lucky speculation.

Like his father, John Brown was a roving jack-of-all-trades; but unlike his father, he believed that nothing could be done without capital and that a poor man must use his capital and borrow. Acting on this theory, he plunged into anything that looked as if it might bring him a quick return on his money. He bought and sold tanneries, he tried his hand at breeding race horses, at sheep raising, farming and speculating in land. Sometimes he prospered. He made money over his tanneries, and he might have done well enough as a farmer, but his unfortunate passion for real estate proved his undoing. The purchase of four farms on credit was the cause of his first collapse, but there were many others.

Brown went through bankruptcy and emerged none the wiser. After the luckless ventures in real estate, he persuaded an agent of the New England Woolen Company of Connecticut to advance him $2,800 to be used for buying wool for the company in Ohio. The Brown family were more than usually in need at the moment, and the $2,800 disappeared in a way Brown could not understand. The woolen company seems to have been an easygoing concern and when, after being put off by promises for several years, they discovered they had been defrauded, they allowed Brown to go through bankruptcy again rather than prosecute him, on the assurance that he would pay something on account from time to time, whenever divine Providence enabled him to do so.

In a country where worldly failure is the unforgivable sin, it was natural enough that the shiftless pioneer should want to cover up his own inability to meet the challenge of civilization by undertaking to avenge the wrongs of others. And yet it would be wrong to deny that this same shiftless pioneer was fiercely honest in his hatred of slavery. In business he had shown himself thoroughly unreliable, if not actually dishonest, but in his private war against slavery he stood foursquare before the world. No doubt he hoped that the fortune which had so far eluded him would somehow fall into his lap when he moved once again, this time into the Territory of Kansas, but this happy-go-lucky attitude toward his private affairs did not interfere with the ruthless war he had declared on everybody and everything associated with slavery.

Not many of those who talked about saving Kansas were as singleminded as John Brown. The mixture of motives among abolitionists was clearly exemplified by Eli Thayer, a prosperous businessman of Worcester, Mass., who organized the Massachusetts Emigrant Aid Society. The purpose of the Society was to raise capital, advertise the advantages of Kansas, recruit well-organized groups of settlers, and send them west equipped with farming tools, bibles, and Sharpe's rifles. The society would help them to build farms, mills, schools and churches. From the investment in lands and buildings Thayer expected to make a handsome profit. As he put it: "When a man does a benevolent deed and makes money at the same time, it merely shows that all his faculties are working in harmony." This unctuous blend of self-interest and philanthropy seems to have satisfied investors. Within a few days of arriving in New York to launch his drive, he obtained pledges of more than $100,000.

A counter-movement was immediately started in Missouri to finance slaveholding settlers. In the year 1856 North and South were both bidding for the Kansas Territory, and the stories of proslavery settlers stuffing the ballot boxes with fraudulent votes in order to win a new State for the South disgusted soberer men than John Brown. Each side included some tough customers, and the natural antagonisms led to ugly incidents. Brown was delighted by the spread of violence. The attack of a proslavery gang upon the town of Lawrence, in which the printing press was destroyed and many of the houses burnt, provided him with all the excuse he needed for taking the law into his own hands. The law that he invoked was the primitive one of "an eye for an eye and a tooth for a tooth." The fact that only one life had been lost in the Lawrence raid, and that by accident, did not deflect him from his grim purpose. Earlier in the year some Free

State men had been killed. Whether their death was due to a quarrel over slavery was not clear, but Brown decided that a balance of lives must be struck. In accordance with his favorite maxim that without the shedding of blood there is no remission of sins, he set out to do God's will.

On the night of May 24, 1856, a small company, made up chiefly of Brown and his sons, descended on a proslavery settlement at Pottawatomie Creek. They were frightened away from the first cabin but at the second, that of the Doyles, a poor family from Tennessee, the father Doyle and two of his sons were dragged out of their cabin and shot or hacked to death. Two other victims from neighboring cabins were butchered in the same way. Not until then was John Brown satisfied that God's will had been done. The only explanation of these unprovoked crimes was that Brown was a maniac. The murdered men were all inoffensive people, but "each one had committed murder in his heart," and he therefore felt justified in "having them killed." Whether or not he did any of the killing himself, he supervised the murders and prided himself on a good night's work.

The events of that night on Pottawatomie Creek were even more far-reaching than Brown had anticipated. Determined as he was to precipitate a war over slavery, he had gone exactly the right way about it by setting men at each other's throats or, as he would have put it, by bringing matters to a head. Slavery men took prompt revenge in what was called the battle of Osawatomie in which one of the Brown sons was killed. Brown accepted his death philosophically. Others would take his place. There was always danger from John Brown's point of view that reason would prevail, that the bogus legislatures would be set aside, that the settlers would leave their rifles and bowie knives at home when they went to the polls, and that they would end by electing a government that honestly represented the people's wishes. This was in fact what actually happened.

As soon as tempers were allowed to cool, the slavery issue in Kansas solved itself. Intelligent Southerners knew perfectly well that their "peculiar system" was already dying out on the fringes of the Cotton Kingdom. In Missouri less than an eighth of the population owned slaves, and further north in the Kansas–Nebraska Territory the prospects for slavery were even less favorable. By 1860 the Free State element had gained control of the legislature, so that slaveholders had left the Territory or sold their slaves outside of Kansas, but by that time John Brown's work was done and the two sections of the country were girding for war.

The folly of fighting and killing for what was bound to come to pass anyway never occurred to him. To rush head-long, destroying whatever lay in his path was the only tactic he understood. Having escaped the hue and cry after the murders on Pottawatomie Creek, he made his way back east to solicit funds for another venture far more desperate than anything he had yet attempted. Kansas had served its turn. It meant nothing to him now except as a blind for the next operation. He was always ready to go back to Kansas, to go raiding over the Missouri border when he was sure there were no troops in the vicinity, to steal horses of proslavery settlers and smuggle their Negroes into Canada, but however popular these raids might be in the parlors of New England abolitionists, Kansas settlers were glad to get rid of him.

Outside of Kansas, where he was regarded as a dangerous nuisance, John Brown of Osawatomie, as he called himself, was well on the way to becoming a hero, at least in antislavery circles. Every Negro he wrested from slavery meant another contribution to the cause. Even more important than the $30,000 he raised for further operations was the honor and consideration he found in the homes of prominent people. In Concord, where he met Emerson and Thoreau, he was acclaimed as "the rarest of heroes, a pure idealist, a man of ideas and principles." With the Concord philosophers setting the tone, it was easy for the "best people" to approve almost any scheme for setting slaves free, no matter how illegal.

Brown preferred not to discuss his next operation in any detail. It was enough for his supporters to know that he was planning an attack on some unnamed point in the South on a much larger scale than anything he had attempted before. During the summer of 1857, he was known to have been conferring in New York with an Englishman, Hugh Forbes, who had fought with Garibaldi in the revolution of 1848. After the collapse of the Roman Republic Forbes drifted to New York, where he supported himself as best he could by giving fencing lessons and translating foreign articles for the *Tribune*. This not too scrupulous adventurer impressed John Brown with his knowledge of guerrilla warfare, and Brown unbosomed himself to him as he was not able to do to anybody else. Here was just the man to train the officers and drill the soldiers of the volunteer company he was planning to raise. While waiting for the volunteers to materialize, Forbes was to be paid a hundred dollars a month for composing a manual on guerrilla warfare. He entered into the undertaking all the more willingly when he found out that a number of well-known and widely respected New England businessmen were behind it. A revolution backed by men of substance was a new experience for one of Garibaldi's Red Shirts.

The band of volunteers, with whose help Brown proposed to overthrow the institution of slavery, consisted of twenty-one men besides himself, sixteen of whom were white and five colored. Most of the whites, including three of his sons, he commissioned as officers in his army. To some of these officers, but not to all, he revealed a prospect that made their Kansas life, the raiding and horse-stealing, seem utterly trivial. He told them that just as God had ordered Moses to deliver the children of Israel from the Egyptians, so God had ordered him, John Brown, to deliver the slaves from bondage.

In view of the magnitude of his plans, Brown was not willing to set forth on this divinely commissioned adventure without some preliminary formalities. Nothing less than a constitutional convention would satisfy him, and at this convention held at Chatham in Upper Canada, not far from Detroit, plans were drawn up for the government of the territory he expected to liberate. None of the Eastern backers were present, and no white man outside of his own party. Chatham was a thriving town of six thousand inhabitants, many of them refugee slaves whom Brown expected to join his army en masse. One Negro finally did speak up: "I b'leve I go wid de ole man"; and four others followed him.

It was one of Brown's many illusions that the free Negroes in Canada and the United States would throw in their lot with him as a matter of course and that the slaves in the Southern States, as soon as they knew of his plans for their liberation, would follow suit. At a given moment the whole South would be ablaze with stampeding Negroes. It would have bewildered John Brown, had he lived to see it, that, when the war he had

138

done so much to bring about finally came to pass, the masters marched off leaving their families and estates in the hands of those same Negroes whom he had tried to incite to rebellion.

Brown's decision to strike at Harper's Ferry was kept a secret from the Eastern backers who believed up to the very end that the money they had raised, and the arms they had supplied him with, were to be used in Kansas. The federal arsenal at Harper's Ferry, a sleepy little town on the borders of Maryland and Virginia where the river Shenandoah joins the Potomac, seemed to make it a strategic goal. By capturing the arsenal and distributing arms and ammunition among the slaves of the neighborhood, he hoped to start a series of slave insurrections. The arsenal and the town itself would become the base of supplies from which the slaves who had revolted were to be armed and supplied.

From there on Brown's plans were hopelessly confused. At one moment he talked of withdrawing into the Allegheny mountains, and founding a colony there in accordance with the provisions of the Chatham constitution. His New England partisans would in the meantime call a Northern convention, restore tranquility and overthrow the proslavery administration. At other times he talked of thrusting his way into the very heart of the South, freeing slaves and gathering hostages wherever he went. During his trial he insisted that he "never did intend murder, or treason, or the destruction of property, or to excite or incite slaves to rebellion, or to make insurrection." This statement is hard to square with the provisions of the constitutional convention, with the careful training in guerrilla warfare, and with the assault on federal property. It would have been more truthful if he had admitted that he was determined to start a revolution against slavery, that he

139

did not know what form the revolution would take, but that by capturing the Harpers Ferry arsenal he had served notice on the United States government of his intentions. What happened afterward was God's affair rather than his. He had planted and watered. God would give the increase.

The taciturn, bearded stranger, calling himself Isaac Smith, who rented the Kennedy farm northeast of Harpers Ferry in the month of July, 1859, spent the next few months awaiting the arrival of certain indispensable "tools." Not until mid-October was he ready to take the momentous step over which he had been brooding for so many years. By that time the various members of the little army had drifted into the farm-house one by one. Most of them had been concealed upstairs and only allowed out at night, so as not to excite too much curiosity in the neighborhood. Except for John Brown himself, no one could quite understand how an assault upon United States property would help to topple over the cursed institution of slavery, but his complete confidence in himself commanded their loyalty. Until he had proved incompetent, as one of them wrote to him, they would sustain his decisions.

On Sunday night, October 16, the sword of Gideon smote Harper's Ferry. John Brown and his band of twenty-one men seized the bridge over the Potomac, cut the telegraph wires and dashed into the sleeping town. At first the raiders had things their own way, and the strategic points were quickly captured. While some of them occupied the arsenal, others drove out into the countryside to round up hostages, set free the slaves and recruit them for the liberating army. One of the first of the gentry to be seized was Colonel Lewis Washington, a great-nephew of the first President. Colonel Washington cherished among his most treasured possessions the sword

presented to his ancestor by Frederick the Great. The surrender of this sword to one of the Negro raiders was a bit of
symbolism upon which Brown set great store. After collecting
a few bewildered slaves, the raiders bundled Washington and
a half dozen other prisoners into a wagon and drove them
back to the arsenal.

So far no blood had been spilled, but John Brown's luck
now deserted him. Several shots had been fired during the
preliminary stages of the raid without taking effect. The first
man to fall, mortally wounded, was the baggagemaster of the
Harper's Ferry station. It is one of the little ironies of history
that this inoffensive citizen was neither a slave owner nor a
slave, but a free Negro respected and liked by the whole
community. The killing of the baggagemaster marked the
turn of the tide. In the confusion that followed, the Baltimore
express, which had been halted outside the station, was allowed
to go through. Soon the whole country knew that the arsenal
had been seized by abolitionists, and the State militia began
converging on the ferry from all directions. Within twenty-
four hours of launching their attack, the surviving raiders were
cut off from all escape. Brown was disappointed that the
Negroes he had come to save showed no desire to avail themselves of the "tools" he had brought for their use.

While the Maryland and Virginia militia were blocking
every exit from the town, they were reinforced by a company
of marines, the only federal troops in the vicinity. President
Buchanan held a hurried conference with his Secretary of
War, as a result of which a certain Colonel Robert E. Lee was
ordered to take command of all troops at Harper's Ferry and
suppress the insurrection. Lee brought with him young J. E. B.
Stuart, a cavalry lieutenant on leave from Kansas. Neither

he nor his commanding officer dreamed of the repercussion on their own lives of the crazy uprising they dealt with so summarily.

Their mission was quickly accomplished. Early on Tuesday morning, Lee sent Stuart to the door of the engine house of the arsenal into which the raiders had now retreated to demand their surrender. Brown tried to argue. He talked of withdrawing from the engine house, provided he were allowed to take his party with him. Some of the prisoners begged that Lee himself would discuss terms with Brown, but Stuart refused to parley. He stepped aside from the door, gave the signal by waving his cap, and the marines came on at the run. Using a heavy ladder as a battering ram, they burst open the door, charged in and overpowered the few remaining defenders. Two of Brown's sons were killed and he himself was wounded, though not as seriously as it appeared at first. If Israel Green, the lieutenant in charge of the storming party, had been wearing a regulation saber instead of a light dress sword, John Brown would have been deprived of his apotheosis. As it was, the blow aimed at him never went home. The blow caught on a belt or a bone, and twisted aside without entering a vital part. The same thrust with a saber would have killed him outright, in which case the John Brown legend would never have been born. His body would have mouldered in the grave, and his soul might or might not have gone marching on, but Mr. Lincoln's army would never have known anything about it.

Within thirty-six hours of occupying the arsenal, Brown himself and four of his men were safely lodged in Charlestown jail. Ten had been killed and the remaining seven had escaped, some temporarily and some for good. The raid had been a complete fiasco. No slaves had joined the raiders of their own accord, and the few who had been impressed were glad to get back to their masters as soon as they were released from the arsenal. Instead of withdrawing into the mountains or leading a triumphal march into the heart of the Southland, Brown dallied as one of his sons prophesied he would, until it was too late. He waited at the base of supplies for the slaves to come in, but they never came. One week after his capture he was placed on trial and six days later, on November 2, he was adjudged guilty of the triple crimes of conspiracy, murder and treason. Judge Parker, who presided over the trial with rigorous impartiality, pronounced the sentence of death by hanging. The date set for the execution was December 2, one month after the day of sentence.

Public opinion in the North complained that the prisoner, not yet recovered from his wounds, was being mercilessly rushed to the gallows, that the sentence of death was a foregone conclusion, and that Virginia had gone mad with fright. What sort of justice could an abolitionist expect in a slave State! Actually Brown was given a scrupulously fair trial. The two lawyers assigned to him as counsel were men of excellent standing in the community and when, during the proceedings, Brown denounced one of them, although he had assured him only the evening before that he was doing for him even more than he had promised, the Court readily admitted to the case a visiting lawyer from the North. As for his wounds, they affected him so little that he was perfectly able to stand up on his feet when he wanted to and deliver a very effective address.

In view of the damning evidence against him, there was only one defense the lawyers could make. When the proceedings opened, counsel had in their hands a telegram from Akron, Ohio, stating that insanity was hereditary in the Brown family. There was ample support for the plea of insanity, but it would have involved Brown in a repudiation of himself, an admission that everything he stood for was meaningless. He preferred the gallows. With the plea of insanity eliminated, the defense could only declare its belief in the nobility of Brown's intentions. The jury listened attentively but the verdict was never in doubt. Considering the swift efficiency of the trial, it is remarkable that the judge should have allowed the condemned man a whole month more of life. It was an invaluable gift, and John Brown made the most of it. No expert in public relations could have presented him to the world as effectively as he presented himself. His dignified conduct in prison, his unswerving belief that he was doing God's will, his unaffected courage displayed in innumerable letters and interviews, redeemed him not only in his own eyes, but in the eyes of the world.

The role of martyrdom, implying as it did a vast posthumous influence, consoled him for a lifetime of failure. The shady business transactions, the bankruptcies, the Kansas murders, would now all be forgotten—not perhaps by everybody, but by most of the articulate people who in the long run make up public opinion. Louisa Alcott talked of "St. John the Just"; Emerson announced that "John Brown would make the gallows glorious like the cross"; and across the ocean Victor Hugo, the spokesman for liberal Europe, thundered his condemnation of America for permitting the execution of so noble a man.

After steeping oneself in all this adulation, it is refreshing to come back to the cool common sense of Abraham Lincoln:

"Old John Brown has been executed for treason against a State. We cannot object, even though he agreed with us in thinking slavery wrong. That cannot excuse violence, bloodshed and treason. It could avail him nothing that he might think himself right."

The execution aroused more publicity than Governor Wise had expected. So frighted was he by the threats of a last-minute rescue that he massed six companies of infantry around the scaffold, together with a detachment of cadets from the Virginia Military Institute. "I had no idea," said Brown, "that Governor Wise considered my execution so important." At the head of the cadets stood a big ungainly man apparently daydreaming, a professor of mathematics soon to be known to the world as Stonewall Jackson. The professor noted that the prisoner refused the services of a chaplain. As a good Christian he prayed for John Brown's soul, but he doubted that the soul of so evil a man could be saved by any prayers.

The beatification of John Brown was not approved by Northerners in general. In any national crisis, the great majority of people demand only to be left alone, but there is always a vocal minority that insists on taking a "strong stand." The fact that John Brown found any defense in the North at all, and that he was even glorified in some quarters, aroused the South to a sense of imminent danger. The Cassandras of "irrepressible conflict" hailed his execution as bringing still nearer the fulfillment of their prophecies. Edmund Ruffin, who had joined the detachment of Virginia cadets for the occasion, distributed the pikes, with which Brown had hoped to arm the slaves, among the Governors of the Southern States. John Brown's pikes would remind those faint-hearted

Southerners who still clung to the Union of the fate in store for them if the abolitionists should ever get their way.

This was exactly what Brown himself wanted. As a monomaniac on the subject of slavery, he had convinced himself that blood must be shed, including, if necessary, his own. If he had been killed in the engine house, if he had escaped from the Charlestown jail, or if Governor Wise of Virginia had been willing to commute his sentence, as he was begged to do even by Southerners, posterity would never have awarded John Brown the martyr's halo. As just another crack-brained abolitionist, the man who made a ridiculous raid on Harper's Ferry, his name would soon have been forgotten, but as the martyr who died to make men free he became perhaps more responsible than any other one man for driving the nation over the precipice.

THREE

The Search for the Middle Way

II

JOHN BROWN'S execution widened the gulf between North and South, but even so the damage was not necessarily irreparable. The "mystic chords of memory," which Lincoln was soon to invoke, still swelled the chorus of the Union. In the campaign of 1860 Breckinridge, the choice of the deep South, did not advocate secession; indeed his supporters in the North urged his election on the grounds that he was more likely than Lincoln or Douglas to avert disunion. There were still plenty of sober-minded men in the North as well as the South who condemned the raid as sedition and treason, and who thought the death penalty was fully justified. Governor Wise of Virginia was ridiculed for posing before the world as the man whose firm policies had saved the nation from disaster, but it was significant that the South also refused to take Governor Wise at his own valuation. In the Republican convention John Brown was specifically repudiated, and no responsible member of the party was ever implicated in any of his activities. Among the abolitionists who had backed him financially and who, in the cases of Gerrit Smith and Samuel Gridley Howe, ran away rather than face a Congressional investigating committee, not one was a bona fide Republican. For a moment after the execution the nation was stunned, and

149

then once again the desire to forget what was unpleasant began to assert itself. After all, John Brown was dead, the orators had had their say about him, and life had to go on. The commercial ties between North and South were stronger than the ideological differences.

The question still puzzling historians is why that spirit of compromise which had so often reconciled the claims of a slaveholding South and a non-slaveholding North failed to operate in 1860. By December of that year it was evident to everybody except a few incurable optimists that the federal Union, the greatest political instrument in the world, was very definitely out of order, and this time there was no Henry Clay to put it together again. When the news reached Charleston that Lincoln had actually been elected, the people of South Carolina decided to have done with the Union once and for all. A Convention was called and on December 20, by a unanimous vote of 169 members, it passed a solemn ordinance declaring that "the union now subsisting between South Carolina and other States, under the name of the 'United States of America,' is hereby dissolved." Within two months of Lincoln's election, delegates from six of the fifteen slave States (South Carolina, Georgia, Alabama, Mississippi, Florida and Louisiana) had met together in Montgomery, Alabama, to launch a new Southern republic.

A number of optimists in the North headed by William H. Seward, the newly appointed Secretary of State, refused to take the secession of the Southern States seriously. Seward chose to believe that secession was a brief madness which would pass away when the people had opportunity for reflection. "Why," said he, "I myself, my brothers and sisters, have all been secessionists—we seceded from home when we were young, but we all went back to it sooner or later. These States will all come back in the same way." As the "Mr. Republican" of his day, Seward was disappointed not to win the Republican nomination, but he was much too keen a politician to sulk in his tent. In preferring Lincoln to Seward, the politicians, as so often happens, had chosen the right man for the wrong reasons. They believed that Seward was so fanatical in his hatred of slavery, that he would antagonize the Border States, whereas Lincoln, while thoroughly sound on the slavery issue, was so likable that he would not antagonize anybody.

Actually Seward was the most accommodating of politicians, far more accommodating than Lincoln. A complex, kindhearted man, he bewildered friends as well as enemies by the ease with which he changed his opinions. The very fact that he did not allow himself the luxury of high principles enabled him to get on with men as different as Charles Francis Adams and Jefferson Davis. On one occasion some years before the war, when the touchy subject of slavery was brought up, Mrs. Davis challenged Seward. "How can you, Mr. Seward, with a grave face, make those piteous appeals for the Negro that you do in the Senate? You surely don't believe the things you say." For a moment he eyed her quizzically, and then with a smile admitted: "I do not. But these appeals, as you call them, have potent effect on the rank and file in the North." Jefferson Davis could not refrain from expressing surprise. "But, Mr. Seward," he said earnestly, "do you never speak from conviction?" "Nev-er," came the frank reply. Davis was aghast. "As God is my judge," he said impulsively, "I never speak from any other motive." Seward put his arm on Davis' shoulder. "I know you do not," he said, "I am always sure of it." The fact was that Seward had become so imbued with the idea that adjustment and concession were the very essence of government that he was never in the least apologetic about advocating a policy of expediency.

Charles Francis Adams, who owed his appointment as Minister to England to Seward and who went along with him politically as much as an Adams could go along with anybody, was so impressed by his adroitness that he never realized what a reckless gambler he was associating with. It was only when the foreign war panacea took possession of Seward that Adams began edging away from him. His *Diary*, into which like his father he confided his inmost thoughts, gradually changed its tone. You could not expect New England probity from a man like Seward. He was nothing but a New York politician, astute enough to scramble to the top of the heap, but quite destitute of the qualities that make for real statesmanship. The *Diary* records nothing about Seward's tortuous course in the Fort Sumter crisis, of which Adams would never have approved. Seward believed that by making a gesture to the South, by which he meant surrendering Fort Sumter, he could win the loyalty of the wavering Border States. They would prove to be the bridge over which the seceded States would return to the fold. So sure was he of the wisdom of this policy and of his ability to carry it out that on March 21 he gave the Southern commissioners to understand that Major Anderson would be withdrawn from Sumter within the next few days. As *The Diary of a Public Man* records, "Much of Mr. Sewards' work must necessarily be done in the dark and through agencies not appreciable by the public at all." Whether he deliberately played fast and loose with the Southerners, or whether he really believed he had converted Lincoln to his point of view, is still a mystery, but when he discovered he could not redeem his pledge he forgot about Sumter and plunged into a new and still more fantastic scheme for restoring the Union.

Seward's talent for improvisation which, between the time of Lincoln's election and the inauguration had served him well, now began to lead him astray. He could flatter himself that he had "brought the ship off the sands," as he wrote to his wife, and that he was now "ready to resign the helm into the hands of the Captain whom the people have chosen." It was true that he had welded the Republican party together and that he had prevented the outbreak of hostilities at Sumter, but he had not yet brought to light that strong Unionist sentiment in the South which he was confident would soon, like a shaft of sunlight, break through the fogs of secession. Before finally resigning the helm into the hands of a man as ignorant of world affairs as Lincoln, he must prove himself the master pilot of his generation. In an evil moment for his reputation as a statesman this small, thin, sallow man with the thick, guttural voice and the everlasting cigar suddenly bethought himself of a foreign war—with Spain, with France, with England, with anybody—as the most effective means of reuniting North and South.

Lord Lyons, the British Minister in Washington, had already warned his government that Seward would be a dangerous foreign minister. "The temptation will be great for Lincoln's party," prophesied Lord Lyons, "if they be not actually engaged in a civil war, to endeavour to divert the public excitement to a foreign quarrel. I do not think Mr. Seward would contemplate actually going to war with us, but he would be well disposed to play the old game of seeking popularity here by displaying violence towards us."

It now remained for Seward to prove how accurately Lyons had anticipated events. On April 1, he submitted to Lincoln that curious document entitled *Some Thoughts for the President's Consideration.* "We are at the end of a month's administration," wrote Seward, "and yet without a policy, either domestic or foreign." For the home policy he proposed to "change the question before the public from one upon slavery or about slavery for a question upon union or disunion." This was to be achieved by trumping up a quarrel with some foreign country and so uniting North and South by involving them in a war against a common enemy.

Lincoln pocketed these extraordinary proposals and nothing more was heard of them until they were published by Nicolay and Hay thirty years later. Seward himself seems to have forgotten the incident. Within a few months, he was telling the British Minister that "the policy of Foreign Governments was founded upon considerations of interest and commerce, while that of the United States was based on high and eternal considerations of principle and the good of the human race."

Whatever mistakes Seward may have made, and certainly his foreign war panacea represents diplomacy at its worst, he was not mistaken in his belief that in spite of all the fanfare over secession the South still cherished kindly feelings toward the Union. The solidarity of the Confederacy during four years of war, and the romance of the lost cause, cannot alter the fact that in every State that seceded the fire-eaters had to overcome the opposition of large minorities. Even in South Carolina, the enthusiasm over secession was not nearly as overwhelming as Barnwell Rhett chose to believe. Nowhere except in Texas were the people given an opportunity to vote directly on the issue of separating from the Union, and in Texas the three-to-one vote in favor of secession was colored by the failure of the federal government to give the western counties adequate protection against the Indians. If the fire-eaters had not been better organized than the "submissionists," as they branded their opponents, they would never have succeeded in stampeding the hastily elected State conventions into secession. As James L. Petigru, the famous "submissionist" of South Carolina, had already foreseen, "the secessionists were afraid to trust the second thoughts of even their own people."

The failure of the Southern loyalists to put up an even better fight than they did is easily explained. Seward was satisfied that secession as an answer to Lincoln's election did not command the support of the Southern people. That may have been true, but even those Southerners most loyal to the Union felt that the South had grievances, and they demanded some assurance from the leaders of the Republican party that those grievances would be met. No such assurance was forthcoming, no friendly gesture was made, no compromise was offered. When the fire-eaters said, "The argument is exhausted. All hope of relief in the Union is extinguished," the conservatives could only shake their heads and reiterate their faith in the good intentions of the Republican party. Unfortunately, by that time good intentions were not enough. "Had they been armed with a reply," says Professor Potter in his searching study of the secession crisis, "they could scarcely have failed to gain the narrow margin of strength which would have enabled them to uphold the Union."

II

The inability of the Southern conservatives to stem the emotional tide was paralleled by a similar failure on the part of the conservatives in the North. If it is true that the Southern fire-eaters had the greatest difficulty in driving their people into secession, it is no less true that the radical Republicans, with the abolitionists in close support, were equally hard put to it to stifle the Northern longing for compromise. Here again, if the people had been given a chance to express themselves, history would have had a different story to tell, but the various peace proposals were never submitted to them. In both sections of the country, the politicians in control were determined not to let the people speak.

Lincoln's election in 1860 did not prove anything very definite about the national attitude toward slavery. The winner polled only 40 per cent of the popular vote, the smallest proportion, incidentally, of any President, and no one can claim that that 40 per cent represented a mandate to reject compromise and embark on a program which might lead to war. Opposition to slavery was only one of the many factors that contributed to the Republican victory. The Germans, whose vote was probably decisive in several northwestern States, were won over by the prospect of free homesteads. Pennsylvanians had been attracted by the promise of a high tariff. Other voters, weary of the long Democratic rule, plumped for a change without stopping to think what the change might imply. As for the 60 per cent who voted against Lincoln, obviously the last thing they wanted was a policy that precluded compromise.

In the first flush of victory, the Republicans were too elated to show any awareness of the storm signals on the horizon. The threat of secession was ignored. Lincoln himself, among others, persisted in his belief that the South was bluffing. According to young Charles Francis Adams, the President-elect spent his time between his election and inauguration "perambulating the country, kissing little girls and growing whiskers." A week after the election, when South Carolina was already on the verge of secession, the New York *Times* reported that "disunion sentiment is rapidly losing ground in the South."

By the time Congress assembled on December 3, the mood had already changed. The election had touched off a panic on the stock exchange, and the business interests reinforced by Northern Democrats and unionists from the Border States were ready to sit down with the Southerners and discuss their grievances. What if the South were not bluffing? Travelers brought back tales from Charleston which seemed to indicate that South Carolina, at least, was in deadly earnest. As the broker of Southern cotton, New York shuddered at the possibility of war. Surely a yearly business of two hundred million dollars was something the politicians had to respect. In the event of war, Southern planters would repudiate their debts and the Northern businessman would be ruined. Under these circumstances, it is not surprising that the business and financial world brought strong pressure to bear on the Republican party to forget about their platform and to make some real effort to conciliate the South. In our own time, we have seen Wall Street held up to obloquy as a warmonger, but in 1860 the rural districts of New England and New York were damning Northern financiers for their unblushing advocacy of peace at any price and "business as usual."

Northern Democrats reminded their Republican friends that though they had won the election, they were still a minority party. They should therefore subordinate their own wishes to the popular demand for a more conciliatory policy. Senator Pugh of Ohio, the same man who had refused to be browbeaten by Yancey at the Charleston Convention, could not be classed as one of the Northern men with Southern principles, yet he now maintained that ninety-nine hundredths of the people were anxious to redress Southern grievances. He favored calling a national convention, in order, if possible, to "lay more deeply, more broadly, and, I trust, more wisely, the foundation of our common liberty and security and happiness." If the American people could not settle their difficulties in a satisfactory manner, there was no hope for mankind anywhere.

All through November and December, the nation waited for some clear definition of policy. President Buchanan, now thoroughly discredited, could only wring his hands and admit his inability to do anything. He denied that a State had the right to secede, and at the same time he denied that the federal government had the right to coerce a State if it should secede. Lincoln, not yet inaugurated, would give the public no inkling of his policy. According to Henry Villard, the able young reporter of the New York *Herald*, he showed "no capacity to grapple manfully with the dangers of this crisis." Villard, who had gone to Springfield to form his own opinion of the new President, gathered that Lincoln felt he could do nothing "to stem the tide of the times."

At this moment, when the authority of the federal government seemed to be crumbling and when Southern senators were already drafting their farewell addresses, a committee of thirteen in the Senate and another committee of thirty-three in the House, one from each State, were eagerly delving into the problem of compromise. The most hopeful of the various schemes proposed was put forward by Senator John J. Crittenden of Kentucky. An impressive, white-haired figure, every inch a Senator, Crittenden was fired by the same passion for compromise, the same belief that everything could be arranged, that had characterized his predecessor, Henry Clay. Born in 1787, while the Constitution was still in the making, he loved the republic with a sentiment peculiar to those who had grown up with it. His colleagues in the Senate admired him for the moderation of his views, his honesty in upholding them and his refusal to tonguelash those who disagreed with him. They admired him also for the "copiousness of his language," an ominous recommendation for a Senator from our point of view, but one that seems to have had a strange appeal for his generation.

Crittenden was the spokesman for the great majority of the nation, the inarticulate masses who had not given up hope of preserving the Union without resorting to war. How could he bring their influence to bear against the little group of extremists North and South who were clamoring for separation, and the still more dangerous "patriots" who insisted that everything had been done that could be done, whose only policy now was to "wait and see." With the spirit of Henry Clay hovering over him, Senator Crittenden was not the man to accept as final any such misplaced stoicism. Even after South Carolina had seceded, he was still bubbling over with compromise proposals. He was enough of a Southerner not to wince over slavery, and at the same time he was far enough removed from the Cotton States, temperamentally as well as geographically, not to be affected by their peculiar States' rights virus. Such a man was obviously anathema to Wendell Phillips and to Yancey, but he was not wrong in thinking that he had the people behind him.

If the Territorial question could only be disposed of, Crittenden was sure everything else would fall into place. He proposed, therefore, to create a western Mason-Dixon line by dividing the area from the Missouri River to California along the line 36° 30′. To the north of that line, slavery would be forever prohibited. To the south it would be not only permitted, but protected, by Congressional legislation. Whenever any area was ready to become a State, it should be admitted free or slave as its people determined. He further proposed that Congress should disclaim the power to abolish slavery where it existed, or to bring up the question of abolition in the District of Columbia, without the permission of Maryland and Virginia. To satisfy the North, Crittenden recommended the maintenance and thorough enforcement of the laws prohibiting the African slave trade, which had become practically a dead letter under the Buchanan administration, and a modification of some of the more objectionable features of the Fugitive Slave Act. Nothing could be done to make the recovery of fugitive slaves palatable to the North, but Crittenden proposed to eliminate at least one peculiarly obnoxious provision of the law by denying the right of a slave owner to summon bystanders to aid in enforcing a warrant for the arrest of a fugitive.

Crittenden wrapped up his series of compromises in a final amendment which forbade any future tampering with the

Constitution in so far as it applied to slavery. By this amendment to prevent amendments, he hoped to banish the slavery question from Congress forever. Had he been able to persuade the Republican members of his committee to accept his bundle of compromises, the history of the next four years would have been very different. "No fact is clearer," says James Ford Rhodes, "than that the Republicans in December defeated the Crittenden compromise; few historic probabilities have better evidence to support them than the one which asserts that the adoption of this measure would have prevented the secession of the cotton States, other than South Carolina, and the beginning of the civil war in 1861." Crittenden's proposals made a deep impression on Northern opinion. Congress was soon flooded with approving memorials, petitions and resolutions, but once again it was a handful of politicians who decided the destinies of the nation, not the people.

Whether they were right in voting as they did, and as Lincoln certainly urged them to do, is another question. In any case the Committee of Thirteen, chosen by Vice-president Breckinridge to consider the Crittenden proposals, included some of the ablest men in the Senate. The Cotton States were represented by Robert Toombs of Georgia and Jefferson Davis. Toombs was often spoken of as a fire-eater but he had not yet shaken the dust of the Union off his feet, and within a few months he was to find himself the only man in the Davis entourage who opposed the firing on Fort Sumter. Davis, already recognized as the leader of the South, was still determined to stave off secession as long as any hope of a peaceable remedy remained. While he had talked a great deal about States' rights, he had so far played no part in planning or hastening the break-up of the Union.

The representatives of the Border States, R. M. T. Hunter, later Secretary of State in the Confederacy, Powell of Kentucky and Crittenden himself, were all dedicated to the task of conciliation. Of the spokesmen for the Northern Democrats, Stephen Douglas was the best known but his colleagues, Bigler of Pennsylvania and Rice of Minnesota, were highly respected in their own communities, and ready like Douglas to support any plan that would relieve the tension. Everything hinged on the sentiments of the Republican members of the committee. This group, headed by Seward, included Jacob Collamer, a quiet-spoken Vermonter, who might well have been won over, and three Northwestern radicals, Ben Wade of Ohio, an abolitionist at heart who joined the committee with the intention of wrecking it, James W. Grimes of Iowa and James R. Doolittle of Wisconsin, who were certainly indifferent, if not actually hostile, to the idea of meeting the South halfway.

At the outset Davis proposed, and the committee agreed, to present no recommendation to the Senate unless it had the support of at least three of the Republicans and five of the other members. Obviously the committee itself must be united if it expected to unite the country. The first vote was taken in Seward's absence and on the vital point at issue—slavery in the Territories—the Republican radicals voted no. When Douglas demanded of them, "Tell us what you do want, what you will do," they remained stonily silent, offering no alternatives whatever. The compromisers counted on Seward to bring his balky colleagues into line. A week before the committee was appointed, Seward had been offered the post of Secretary of State, and that fact in itself raised Crittenden's hopes. No one knew much about Lincoln's views on the subject of compromise, but Seward was generally believed to be in favor of a moderate policy. He had traveled far since his speech as a Senator in 1848 when he told an audience in Cleveland that slavery must be abolished, "and you and I must do it." His talk about an irrepressible conflict was generally thought to have cost him the Republican nomination, and his recent speeches seemed to indicate that he was ready to surrender any point or principle to hold the Union together. Had not his faithful friend and political crony, Thurlow Weed, recommended restoring the Missouri Compromise Line, and was not that the essence of the Crittenden proposals?

It is not surprising, therefore, that the conservatives on the committee were still hopeful. The Compromise had to go through. Toombs and Davis may have been restive, but if they were sure the Republicans would not only vote for the Compromise but support it vigorously in Congress they would go along with them. Everything depended on Seward. As the acknowledged leader of the party, he would probably be able to swing the other Republicans into line. More important even than that, his approval of the Compromise would indicate that the President too was in favor of a conciliatory policy. Seward's position at this moment was certainly not an easy one. Lincoln had offered him the most important post in the Cabinet, a post which he felt he could not refuse, yet he had no idea what policy Lincoln meant to pursue. Would he stand firmly on the Chicago platform and not yield an inch on the question of slavery in the Territories, in which case Mississippi, Florida, Georgia and Alabama were bound to join South Carolina in secession, or would he leave it to his Secretary of State to work out some way of holding these States in the Union?

Believing that any compromise was preferable to war or

disunion, Seward had sent his henchman, Thurlow Weed, to Springfield to take the necessary soundings and to persuade Lincoln, if possible, to accept a division of the Territories along the lines Crittenden had suggested. Weed arrived in Springfield the day the South Carolina Convention passed its Ordinance of Secession. There is no record of his conversation with Lincoln, but presumably he stressed the arguments that were already making headway among conservative Republicans in the East. The secession of South Carolina, long foreseen, was not necessarily a disaster. Provided her example were not followed, South Carolina would sooner or later have to return to the Union, but "if," as the New York *Tribune* said, "eight States having five millions of people choose to separate from us they can not be permanently withheld from so doing by Federal cannon." Either there must be concessions or the erring sisters must be allowed to depart in peace.

Lincoln refused to be impaled on either horn of this dilemma. So strong was his faith in the common sense of the people that he could not bring himself to belief in the imminence of the crisis. Douglas once said of Lincoln that he was eminently a man of the atmosphere which surrounds him. The atmosphere of Springfield was one of boundless confidence in the ability of the Republican party to ride out the storm without having to hoist signals of distress. Lincoln therefore had no hesitation in rejecting Weed's overtures. He still thought that if all those who had voted for him stood their ground without wobbling the danger would blow over. "Let there be no compromise on the question of extending slavery," he wrote to his friend Lyman Trumbull. "Have none of it. Stand firm. The tug has to come, and better now than at any other time."

Lincoln made it clear to Weed that his views were not for publication. At the same time, Seward was to know about them and to record his vote accordingly. The committee met again, this time with Seward, on Christmas Eve. Instead of persuading his Republican colleagues to change their minds, as Crittenden hoped he would do, Seward of course voted with them. He also took the opportunity to introduce a number of innocuous proposals of his own dealing with the enforcement of the Fugitive Slave Act, but this was not what Southerners wanted. Nothing would satisfy them but the right, guaranteed by constitutional amendment, to carry slavery into the Territories. This right, which would not have amounted to anything, since the remaining Territories were not suited to slavery, and since the Southern settlers would always have been outnumbered as they had been in Kansas, Lincoln refused to grant. Toombs immediately telegraphed the Georgia newspapers that the Republicans had defeated the Crittenden amendments, and that by so doing they had left the South no alternative but secession. Douglas now made one last proposal, which the conservatives approved, but this was of no consequence in view of the united opposition of the Republican group. Toombs then moved that the committee report that they could not agree upon any proposals, and asked to be discharged.

So ended the most hopeful of the many attempts made to avert disunion and war. As the New York *Tribune* said: "Mr. Crittenden's proposal is the most considerate and conciliatory of any that have been suggested by our opponents; and if we could concede to any one he would be the man. We all know Mr. Crittenden to be a true Unionist and a patriot." (Dec. 31, 1860) Unfortunately Mr. Crittenden, with all his virtues, was not Henry Clay. The fanatics had been hard at work since 1850 driving men into positions from which they could not retreat. Something had to break, either the Republican party or the Union. The Republican party proved the stronger of the two.

III

The House committee of Thirty-three was, if anything, even less successful than the Senate committee had been. The Northern Democrats were not represented at all, and the members chosen from the Border States were not men of any standing. Thus the committee included no one whose heart was really set on reaching an amicable agreement. The Southerners had already made up their minds that the Republicans would concede nothing that would satisfy them and the Northerners, under the leadership of Charles Francis Adams, used the committee as a means of demonstrating to some of their weak-kneed brethren that every concession to the Southern point of view led to a demand for more. The committee's final report has been compared to the mountain laboring to bring forth a mouse. It embodied a series of innocuous proposals but, as none of these commanded a majority of the members, Congress paid no attention to them.

In spite of these setbacks the Northern friends of compromise were not yet ready to give up the fight. Douglas and Crittenden could not believe that the Republicans would be content just to stand firm and do nothing. If the people could only be given a chance to vote on his proposals, Crittenden was sure they would be carried by an overwhelming majority. The number of petitions endorsing the plan, submitted to

Congress during the month of January, 1861, while it was still a live issue, suggests that he may well have been right. Even Horace Greeley, a bitter opponent of the Compromise, admitted some years after the war that many Republicans and all Democrats were in favor of it. Naturally the radical Republicans were opposed to a popular referendum and, because of their obstruction, it never came to a vote in the Senate. Like the noisy secessionists in the Cotton States, they did not dare let the people speak.

Douglas, who was more of a fighter than Crittenden, pressed home the fearful alternatives to compromise. Any political party which refused to allow the people themselves to determine between revolution and war, on the one side, and "obstinate adherence to a party platform on the other," assumed a fearful responsibility. As he saw it, the nation faced three choices, compromise, peaceable separation, or war. It seemed to him inconceivable that sensible men should not prefer to explore all the possibilities of the first choice before resigning themselves to either of the other two. There was no question involved of loyalty to the Union. As events proved, neither Douglas nor Crittenden hesitated for a moment in rallying to Lincoln's side as soon as war was declared. Douglas indeed thought that Lincoln made a mistake in not calling for 200,000 men at once instead of 75,000. To Crittenden's great sorrow, one of his sons threw in his lot with the Confederacy and rose to be a general in the Confederate army. The other son became a general on the Union side. Crittenden's prophecy of a brothers' war was thus all too literally realized.

One last-minute effort at compromise, the Virginia-inspired Peace Convention, showed that the Border States had not yet succumbed to the frenzy of the fire-eaters or to the quieter but no less irreconcilable demands of the Northern radicals. The chasm between the two was widening day by day, but a few elder statesmen in the Border States thought that the waters of bitterness might still be bridged. On February 4, 1861, after seven States had already seceded, the commissioners to a Peace Convention met together in Washington. The moving spirit behind this forlorn enterprise was the venerable ex-President, John Tyler of Virginia. Tyler had persuaded the Virginia state legislature to issue a call to all States, "whether slaveholding or non-slaveholding . . . to unite with Virginia in an earnest effort to adjust the present unhappy controversies." To make sure that the shooting did not begin while the commissioners were still deliberating, President Buchanan and the Governors of the seceded States were begged to abstain pending the proceedings from any acts "calculated to produce a collision of arms between the States and the Government of the United States."

This pathetic appeal proves how desperate the situation was. Actually the Convention was doomed before it even got under way. Delegates from the seceded States met in Montgomery to form their own government on the very day that the Peace Convention assembled in Washington. Naturally they refused to take any part in the Peace Convention beyond assuring Tyler of their peaceful intent coupled with an inflexible determination to maintain their independence. Most of the Northern commissioners accepted Virginia's invitation only with the idea of preventing a compromise. Michigan, Wisconsin and Minnesota did not respond at all. Senator Chandler of Michigan would have been in favor of sending "stiff-backed" men if there had been any likelihood of the Republicans caving in, but that particular danger did not arise.

Chandler was one of the Northern fire-eaters who wanted to get down to business as soon as possible. The Union needed "a little bloodletting," and he would welcome it. Some of the Republican delegates might have preferred compromise to civil war, but they were in a minority in their State delegations. The radicals took the line that there was no need for a Peace Convention. It had been summoned "to afford to the people of the slaveholding States adequate guarantees for their rights." No one was threatening the rights of the South, and the Convention was therefore merely a scheme of the slaveholding interests to extort concessions which they had failed to win at the polls. As long as Northerners insisted on inflexible adherence to the Chicago platform and refused even to discuss what it meant, all hope of peace was over. James Russell Lowell, speaking for the abolitionists, reported in the *Atlantic Monthly* that "the usual panacea of palaver was tried," with the usual negative results. The Convention remained in session exploring various paths to compromise until Inauguration Eve, but Congress found nothing in its proposals worthy of serious consideration.

The only man who really profited by the Peace Convention was the bustling, harassed but resourceful, Secretary of State. Mr. Seward was still playing for time. Although the compromise plans had failed, both in the Senate and in the House, and although Senator Wade had made a most unfortunate speech in Congress announcing he "had supposed we were all agreed that the day of compromises was at an end," Seward could still insist, thanks to the Convention, that conciliatory measures were in progress, and that no State ought to secede until every avenue of compromise had been explored. Seven slave States had already gone out of the Union. This was a

serious blow to the nation, but Seward did not consider it
fatal. If enough of the remaining eight slave States could be
kept within the fold, he was convinced that the new-born
Confederacy would very soon collapse. He set himself, therefore, to divide the South by conciliating the Border States,
particularly Virginia and Maryland, and holding them loyal
until the tide of reaction set in. For this purpose the "palaver"
ridiculed by James Russell Lowell was invaluable. People will
not go to war as long as they can be persuaded to keep on
talking with each other. By giving his approval to the Peace
Convention, and by encouraging the delegates to talk at great
length, which was not difficult—the official report of the
debates fills 621 pages—Seward succeeded in delaying secession in Virginia, North Carolina and Tennessee, and preventing it in Maryland, Kentucky and Missouri. Delaware, the
remaining slave State, was never in danger. The Delaware
legislature passed resolutions endorsing the Crittenden amendments and strongly urged their approval by Congress, but it
expressed unqualified disapproval of secession.

To that extent Seward was successful, but there was one
element in the atmosphere of Union sentiment and secessionist
sympathy pervading the Convention which Seward, and perhaps Lincoln too, failed to take into account. The word
"Unionist" was a chameleon word that changed its color in
different parts of the country. In South Carolina a Unionist
meant a submissionist, a man who would submit to any indig-
nity rather than fight for his rights. In North Carolina or
Virginia, a Unionist became a hard-headed, independent fellow who would not be stampeded into secession just to please
South Carolina. He recognized secession as a legitimate
weapon but he would use it only in the last resort, after every

appeal to reason had failed. Finally, in the Northern States a Unionist was, quite simply, a man who regarded secession as treason.

When Seward relied on the latent Union sentiment in the South to extinguish the rebellion, he was really fooling himself. By the time Lincoln was inaugurated, seven States had already decided that they had the right to secede. The question now was, how could the dry rot be stopped, how could those who had made the great decision, as well as those who were wavering, be brought back into the family? This question the 36th Congress had failed to consider. It passed out of existence without providing for the reconstruction of the Union by conciliation or by coercion.

The Union men of the upper South assumed that the hesitancy over reinforcing Anderson in Fort Sumter indicated a genuine peace policy, and they were encouraged in that belief by members of the Cabinet. To those optimists who persisted in thinking that the new administration was bound to realize that the principles of the Republican party were not the principles of the majority of the Northern people, Lincoln's inaugural address was like a douche of cold water. The country had heard nothing from him since the Cooper Union speech. He had spoken a few times in the course of his leisurely tour from Springfield to Washington, but he had deliberately avoided any full statement of policy. "I have kept silence," he said, "for the reason that I supposed it was peculiarly proper that I should do so until the time came when, according to the custom of the country, I could speak officially." He had made known his position to a few friends and counselors, but the country as a whole knew little about him. Southern fire-eaters pictured him as an abolitionist orang-outang, a description which unfortunately was more likely to stick in the public mind than the mild statement of Alexander Stephens that Lincoln "was not a bad man." Indeed, Stephens thought "Lincoln is just as good, safe and sound a man as Mr. Buchanan."

In spite of the conciliatory language in which it was couched, Lincoln's inaugural address made it perfectly clear that he had no intention of compromising on any of the critical issues. He would not surrender Fort Sumter, as the Virginia Unionists hoped he might do. On the contrary he would maintain it as a symbol of the vitality of the Union. He would not admit that the South had any grievances, and he would never recognize the right of secession. The Union was permanent. The power confided to him by the American people would accordingly "be used to hold, occupy and possess the property and places belonging to the government, and to collect the duties and imposts..." At the same time he promised faithfully to enforce the provisions of the Fugitive Slave law, and he was even prepared to approve an amendment to the Constitution to the effect that "the Federal Government shall never interfere with the domestic institutions of the States, including that of persons held to service."

These were not the real points at issue, as Lincoln must have known. On the much more controversial question of slavery in the Territories, Lincoln gently but firmly shut the door in the face of the compromisers. A State was not the judge of the extent of its grievances and of the mode and measure of redress. In all disputes with the federal government, a State must abide by the decision of the government. The implication was clear. The Republican party was in power and it intended to use that power to further its own aims.

To the victors belong the spoils. There was nothing belligerent about the tone of the address. Lincoln deprecated war and hoped to avoid it if he could, and yet anybody listening to the speech carefully could have caught the far off clank of metal. The very fact that he denied the existence of grievances in the South must have been profoundly discouraging to the Unionists in the Border States. They noted the outstretched hand bearing an olive branch but they noted also that the other hand, in which they were more interested, was empty. Lincoln was just as ready to override the compromisers in the North as the fire-eaters had been to override the submissionists in the South.

IV

During the few weeks that elapsed between the inauguration and the firing on Fort Sumter, Lincoln's time and energy were largely absorbed by officeseekers. He was said to be making all the appointments himself, undertaking to handle "the whole patronage small and great leaving nothing to the Chiefs of Departments." Assuming this to be true, and it may very well have been, since no President ever operated the political machine more skillfully than Lincoln, the muddle over Fort Sumter becomes more understandable. Lincoln never quite made up his mind about Sumter. Events moved too quickly for him. "My policy is to have no policy," he once said to John Hay, which explains why Gideon Welles, the Secretary of the Navy, complained that he was kept as much in the dark about Lincoln's plans and views as any outsider. The New York *Times* of March 21 considered that the true policy of the government was one of "masterly inactivity," meaning that if the government did nothing to antagonize them the people in the South would eventually return to their senses. In a time of crisis, a policy of masterly inactivity is hardly likely to be popular, and it is not surprising that the public soon began to feel that under Lincoln the country was drifting just as aimlessly as under Buchanan.

Nothing points up the *opéra bouffe* confusion within the administration more strikingly than the two sets of orders issued simultaneously to two different naval officers to take command of one of the most powerful vessels in the navy, and to embark at once on two separate missions. Seward, in the President's name, ordered Lieutenant David Porter to take command of the *Powhatan* and to proceed at once to the reinforcement of Fort Pickens in Florida. Pickens was the only other fort besides Sumter still in government hands. This was done without the knowledge of the Secretary of the Navy. At the same time the President approved of orders signed by Welles designating the *Powhatan* as the flagship of an expedition to provision Fort Sumter. Lincoln had apparently signed the orders drafted by Seward without reading them.

The *Powhatan* muddle is significant for several reasons. It shows that a month after his inauguration Lincoln was still vacillating as to what to do about Sumter—whether to evacuate it, reinforce it, or merely provision it. It shows too that Seward, under the illusion that he was premier, was meddling in army and navy affairs. He had decided that Sumter should be given up to please the Virginia Unionists, and that Pickens should be held as the symbol of federal authority. Without consulting anybody, he took what seemed to him the necessary steps to put this decision into effect.

For Lincoln there were other issues involved besides the

appeasement of Virginia Unionists. He had promised to hold, occupy and possess the property and places belonging to the government. Tremendous pressure was being brought to bear upon him by the radical Republicans not to give in. On the other hand, the business interests in the country were clamoring for a peaceful solution of all difficulties. And not only the business interests. Neal Dow, the famous prohibition champion of Maine and later a general in the Union army, assured the President that "the evacuation of Fort Sumter would be fully approved by the entire body of Republicans in this State —and I doubt not in all the country."

Nor could Lincoln forget the popular interest in the Crittenden Compromise proposals, or the importance of not doing anything to alienate the Border States. Perhaps he would have surrendered Sumter in exchange for an assurance of the unswerving loyalty of Virginia. "A State for a fort is no bad business," he is reported to have said but the offer, if it was ever made, came too late.

In the end the President straddled the issue by deciding to provision the fort without reinforcing it. At the same time he dispatched a note to the Governor of South Carolina informing him that the troops in the expedition would not be landed unless the provisioning should be resisted, or the fort fired upon. This note precipitated the issue. In spite of the assurances of Southern agents in Washington, founded on Seward's promises, that Sumter would be evacuated from one day to the next, the Stars and Stripes still flew over Charleston Harbor. Southern patience could bear it no longer. After a flurry of consultation with the local authorities, President Davis, fearful that the hotheaded fire-eaters in Charleston might override his authority if he did not act quickly, ordered General Beauregard, the Confederate commander in Charleston, to demand the surrender of the fort and if the demand was refused to "reduce it."

Major Anderson, as all the world knows, found it impossible to comply with these demands and on the morning of April 12 the Palmetto Guards of South Carolina, the flower of Southern chivalry, accorded to Edmund Ruffin, the oldest and most fanatical fire-eater of them all, the distinction of firing the first gun of the Civil War. Thus after thirty years of agitation and obstruction the warmongers, North and South, could sit back and relax. The last possibility of compromise had been eliminated. Up until that moment Garrison and Wendell Phillips, representing the radical wing of the Abolitionist party, had been clamoring for separation from the South. "Who would not prefer living in a house of moderate dimensions in peace, to dwelling in a mansion in a daily bitter and empoisoning strife?" That was the official line, but within twenty-four hours it was conveniently forgotten. The spirit of disunion which they had championed so vigorously had suddenly been transformed into an evil thing. Secession had become "the concentration of all diabolism."

Meanwhile the great bulk of the abolitionist army had thrown itself into the arms of the Republican party. The professional politicians were not pleased with their new allies but they could not ignore them. Lincoln himself was always careful not to offend the antislavery radicals. It was true that as a young man, in 1837, he joined in a formal written protest stating that "slavery is founded on both injustice and bad policy but that the promulgation of Abolitionist doctrines tends rather to increase than abate its evils." By 1860, even though he was not ready to proclaim any permanent alliance with abolitionists, he was more than ready to accept their support. Such men as Wade and Sumner, not to mention Garrison and Wendell Phillips, had laid hold of a principle without which the republic could not exist—the principle of free discussion. Lincoln could not help being drawn to men who clung so tenaciously to things he too considered all-important.

Meanwhile the incessant agitation of the abolitionists had increased the evils of slavery. There had been no laws against teaching slaves to read and write until the abolitionist movement was well under way. Inevitably the lot of the slave grew harder as the antislavery crusaders stepped up their campaign. There was a natural tendency among slaveholders to draw the rein tighter whenever rumors of rebellion swept the land, and to rely more and more on the power of fear. Rightly or wrongly, the instigation to rebel was always attributed to the abolitionists. At the same time in certain parts of the North, particularly in Ohio and in New England, pity for the slave had generated a tremendous moral force which implemented the program of the Republican party. As a politician who hungered for office and as an essentially kindly man who deplored human bondage, Lincoln must have given serious thought to the abolitionist movement. No doubt he observed that William Lloyd Garrison and those who stood with him were a small group without serious political influence, but he must also have noted that the non-Garrisonian abolition movement, although it never acquired any standing as an independent political force, was beginning to make itself felt in the councils of the two major parties. When the Whig abolitionists of New York State brought about the defeat of

Henry Clay in the presidential campaign of 1844, the lesson was obvious. Practical politicians could no longer afford to disregard abolition sentiment.

V

While Lincoln was still an obscure Congressman, the struggle in Congress over antislavery petitions and the use of mails for abolitionist literature had already declared itself. John Quincy Adams who, as President of the United States, had shown himself a very halfhearted fighter in the antislavery cause, and who had turned a deaf ear to all Great Britain's appeals for co-operation in the suppression of the slave trade, suddenly became excited about slavery when he saw that the Southern members in Congress would deny to the people the ancient right of petition. To the day of his death, Adams was never especially concerned over the plight of the slave. His defiant protest over the gag resolution, for which he earned the sobriquet "Old Man Eloquent," was aroused by his sense that the abolitionists were fighting indirectly for the rights of white men as well.

The controversy over gag rule was not quite the clear-cut conflict between right and wrong that Adams made it appear. Inspired by Theodore Weld, who kept himself very much in the background, abolitionists all over the country flooded Congress with endless antislavery petitions. If these had been received and dealt with in the usual way, they would have clogged the whole machinery of government. With great skill the abolitionists finally goaded Congress into passing what came to be known as the gag resolutions. These resolutions established the rule that all petitions on the subject of slavery should be laid on the table without being printed, referred, or further acted upon. Southerners may have looked upon this ruling as a temporary expedient made necessary by the action of fanatics, but in the eyes of the world they appeared to be denying one of the most sacred rights of democracy. On the other hand, the abolitionists, who had hitherto been regarded, at least in conservative circles, as irresponsible agitators, were now transformed into the indomitable champions of free speech.

Lincoln was attracted to the antislavery party for the same reason as John Quincy Adams. While he may have been more troubled than Adams by "the monstrous injustice of slavery," his first thought was for the white man. The Negro was secondary. Lincoln's consciousness of the pernicious effect of slavery on American society explains his pathetic faith in the policy of colonization. For a long time he toyed with the idea of freeing the slaves by slow stages, and then settling as many as could be induced to leave the country in Liberia, Mexico, or South America. During the war, when he was struggling to make up his mind about emancipation, he assured Congress that it would not lower standards of white labor even if the freedmen were not deported. But if they were deported, "enhanced wages to white labor is mathematically certain. . . . Reduce the supply of black labor by colonizing the black laborer out of the country, and by precisely so much you increase the demand for, and wages of, white labor." Again in his plea to the representatives of the Border States, in July 1862, to emancipate their slaves by selling them to the nation, he virtually promised them that the freed Negroes would not become an encumbrance. "Room in South America for colonization can be obtained cheaply and in abundance, and when the numbers shall be large enough to be company and encouragement for one another, the freed people will not be so reluctant to go."

Lincoln's concern for the well-being of the American people, was certainly one, if not the chief, reason for his refusal to accept the Crittenden Compromise. He insisted that the settlers in the Territories had a right to "a clean bed with no snakes in it." Lincoln might not have admitted it but to many of his supporters "snakes" referred not only to the existence of slavery, but to the presence of free Negroes as well. There is no greater fallacy than the assumption that the majority of Republicans were moved by a spirit of warm, human sympathy for the Negro. In 1853 the State of Illinois was legally closed to Negro immigration, free or slave, and it never occurred to Lincoln or to anybody else that the law should be changed. In Kansas, free-soilers, while they were still struggling with border ruffians, drafted an antislavery constitution which forbade free Negroes to set foot in the State, and in Missouri Frank Blair, one of Lincoln's staunchest supporters, chose as the motto for his paper, "White Men for Missouri and Missouri for White Men." Such sentiments cannot have been pleasing to simon pure abolitionists, but they could afford to let them go since Lincoln did not openly approve of them.

There were other reasons besides the ultimate welfare of the American people for resisting the pressure to accept the Crittenden proposals. Lincoln did not believe that the Crittenden Compromise, or any other compromise, would relieve the tension. Nor did he believe, as Douglas and Crittenden did, that the rejection of the Compromise necessarily meant war. Even though he persistently underestimated the threat of secession, it does not follow that if he had accepted any of the compromises offered the secession movement would have been arrested, or that the war could have been avoided. Lincoln was dealing with fanatics. The fire-eaters did not want to be conciliated any more than the abolitionists, and they would have done everything in their power to vitiate the Compromise. As for the abolitionists, the Garrisonians hated the Union and therefore could not have been tempted by any move to preserve it, least of all one that involved placating the South. In that respect, they agreed with good political abolitionists like Wade and Sumner who would not have hesitated to wreck any policy savoring of appeasement.

Another factor to be considered was the possibility that the South would use any compromise as a starting point for a new series of filibustering expeditions. Pierce and Buchanan had both worked hard to add Cuba to the national domain as another slave State, and though their efforts were thwarted by Congress, Southerners still talked about the necessity of extending the empire of slavery. Barnwell Rhett, a fitting spokesman for the expansionists, dreamed of a mighty empire reaching "across this continent to the Pacific, and down through Mexico to the other side of the great gulf, and over the isles of the sea. . . ." Lincoln might well have argued that since the attempts to realize this fantasy had failed under such weak Presidents as Pierce and Buchanan they were not likely to succeed under his vigorously antislavery administration, but he preferred to take no chances. The containment of slavery was not a matter for compromise.

As a politician as well as a moralist, Lincoln knew that he could not yield. "Surrender," as he wrote to a fellow Republican just before leaving Springfield, would be "the end of us." Successful candidates have sometimes been known to kick away the platform by which they mounted to office, but Lincoln was not one of them. The Republican platform suited him and he meant to abide by it. Despite all the nonsense talked about them in the South, the Republicans who nominated Lincoln were not wild men, and the platform they drafted was not a radical document. Four years earlier, at the instigation of Frémont, the newly formed Republican party had deliberately set out to antagonize the South by coupling slavery with polygamy, and branding them both as "twin relics of barbarism." There was nothing of that kind in the platform of 1860. As far as possible, it tried to ingratiate itself with the South by denouncing John Brown's invasion as the "gravest of crimes," and recognizing the right of each State to order "its own domestic institutions" (a euphemism for slavery) as it chose. At the same time, it denied "the authority of Congress, or of a Territorial legislature, to give legal sanction to Slavery in any Territory of the United States."

Lincoln was satisfied with the platform. Quite naturally, he chose to ignore the fact that from the Southern point of view it was a deceptive document cunningly contrived to please the radicals as well as the conservatives. That is hardly surprising since it is always the duty of a platform committee to conciliate the warring tribes within the party. It was because the Democrats forgot this great truth at their convention in Charleston that the Democratic party wandered in the wilderness for thirty years. The Republicans, being out to win the election rather than demonstrate their intellectual honesty, were better advised. To please the conservatives, they promised not to interfere with slavery where it already existed, and to cater to the abolitionists they inserted into the platform the "all men are created equal" passage from the Declaration of Independence.

Such discrepancies were of no great importance. The public soon forgets the platform in its interest in the candidate, but in this case the candidate gave them no satisfaction. To a few friends he wrote letters carefully marked "private and confidential," in which he expressed his views very clearly, but the public was left in the dark. He made no campaign speeches and wrote only one short public letter, in which he expressed his approval of the Chicago Platform. While Lincoln always insisted that anyone who wanted to know where he stood on any of the great questions of the day had only to read his speeches, this was not quite true. His statements on controversial questions were not always consistent.

During the Mexican War, he had declared that "Any people anywhere being inclined and having the power have the right to rise up and shake off the existing government, and form one that suits them better." Such a statement, even admitting the proviso "having the power," is hard to square with his denial of the right of secession. Again, in his debates with Douglas, he said in one speech (July 10, 1858) that we should "discard all this quibbling" about men or races being inferior and should "once more stand up declaring that all men are created equal." In another speech (September 18, 1858) he claimed that he was not, and never had been, "in favor of bringing about in any way the social and political equality of the white and black races." Nor was he in favor of making voters or jurors of Negroes, or of allowing them to hold office. He believed that there were certain physical differences which "will forever forbid the two races living together on terms of social and political equality."

Other statesmen have been involved in far more embarrassing contradictions, but the South was not unreasonable in demanding that Lincoln should clarify his position. Of course what the South wanted him to say was something he could not possibly have said without breaking up the Republican party, and probably losing his own self-respect as well. If he had been prepared to denounce the abolitionists and all their works, and if at the same time he had thrown himself heart and soul into the task of persuading Northern Senators to accept the Crittenden Compromise, he might have headed off secession and avoided the war, but loyalty to his party forbade it, quite apart from his own instincts.

Fortunately for Lincoln the two coincided. Through his partner, William Herndon, Lincoln was well advised of abolitionist activities. Herndon was an abolitionist at heart. He bought all the books and pamphlets on the subject that he could lay his hands on, and he and Lincoln devoured them together. While he was never able to imbue Lincoln with his own fiery zeal, or with the rancor that inspired Sumner or Wendell Phillips, Herndon confirmed Lincoln in his hatred of slavery, and in his conviction that any compromise ignoring either the ethical or the political issues involved was bound to fail. Lincoln never lost sight of these two equally important aspects of the slavery problem. Most of his contemporaries, assuming they disapproved of slavery at all, concentrated on one or the other. On the matter of the Union, for instance, he and Douglas thought alike. The breach that developed between them was due to Douglas' moral obtuseness. He was so much the 100 per cent American, so consumed with his desire to see the nation grow and prosper, that he would not allow anything, even slavery, to stand in the way. The abolitionists looked at the national scene through the other end of the telescope. They were so aghast at the immediate injustice of slavery that they could not discern the political background.

Lincoln had to broaden the horizon of the politicians at the same time that he was teaching the abolitionists the facts of political life. The abolitionists never liked him and, being themselves politically inept, they distrusted his skill in practical politics. Wendell Phillips at one time called him "the slavehound of Illinois," but Lincoln never protested and at the end of the war he gave the abolitionists credit, and more than credit, for their contribution to the final victory. Indeed he went so far as to say that "the logic and moral power of Garrison and the antislavery people of the country have done all." Though Lincoln's instincts may have drawn him toward the abolitionists, his intelligence reminded him that his first allegiance was to his party. He had not been active in the founding of the Republican party and he had shown no enthusiasm over Frémont, the first Republican standard bearer. Frémont's qualities, such as they were—a love of adventure and an impulsiveness verging on insubordination—were not qualities that appealed to a cautious politician like Lincoln. But if he was a latecomer into the new party, once he had made the great decision he never looked back. Having watched the Whigs crumble to pieces before his eyes, he had to seek his political fortune elsewhere. Herndon, who knew Lincoln better at this time of his life than anybody else, once described his ambition as as "a little engine that knew no rest."

Henceforth that little engine would be used exclusively to operate the Republican machine.

Lincoln seized on the Dred Scott decision as proving, if further proof were necessary, that the slavery issue was irrepressible. In rendering his memorable decision, Chief Justice Taney unconsciously flung down a challenge to the virility of the still youthful Republican party. If it had been ignored, the party would probably have disintegrated, but Lincoln pounced on it and for the next three years, until he was nominated for President, the Dred Scott decision dominated every speech he made.

VI

Dred Scott was a typically shiftless, illiterate slave, who never understood the role he was destined to play in American history. He belonged originally to a certain Captain Peter Blow, whose descendants seem to have felt some responsibility for him and looked after him long after he had passed out of their hands. Shortly after Blow's death he was purchased by Dr. John Emerson, a surgeon in the United States army, who was stationed in St. Louis. When he was transferred to a post in Illinois, and later into the Wisconsin Territory, Dr. Emerson took Dred with him as his body servant. After living for three years in the Territory, the Emerson family returned with Dred Scott, still a slave, to their home in St. Louis. Scott made no protest at the time but a few years later, under abolitionist auspices, he sued for his freedom on the grounds that his residence in the Territory of Wisconsin, where slavery was forbidden, automatically transformed him into a free man.

In the meantime Dr. Emerson had died and his widow had married Dr. Charles Chaffee, a Massachusetts abolitionist who was elected to Congress shortly after their marriage. Nothing would have been easier than for Mrs. Chaffee and her husband to have given Dred his freedom, but instead they arranged a fictitious sale of the Negro and his family to Mrs. Chaffee's brother, John F. A. Sanford of New York. A group of abolitionists then started suit against Sanford to obtain Scott his freedom. Since he was already in antislavery hands, the real object of the suit was to evoke a decision at the highest level as to whether a Negro was entitled to the rights of federal citizenship. The case was argued in a federal court in Missouri, which found in favor of Sanford. As expected and prearranged, the case was then appealed to the Supreme Court.

Two days after the inauguration of Buchanan, the eighty-year-old Chief Justice, Roger Brooke Taney, rose to read his opinion in the case of *Sanford vs. Scott*. A Marylander, who as a young man had set free the few slaves he had inherited, Taney was anything but the pliant tool of the slave interests that Lincoln believed him to be. He had even gone on record as declaring that slavery was "a blot on our national character," a blot that he hoped to see eventually wiped away. But as a judge, he felt he should be guided not by what his conscience told him was right, but by what he believed the law required him to decide. By a six-to-three majority, the Court declared that Negroes were not citizens of any State, and hence not citizens of the United States. Therefore, not being a citizen, Scott had no right to sue in a Federal Court.

If Taney had left it at that, Dred Scott's name would soon have been forgotten. As the lazy, goodnatured porter of Barnum's Hotel, St. Louis, he would have been an object of interest and curiosity to the guests, but he would never have become a household word along with Uncle Tom and John Brown. Unfortunately Taney, anticipating dissenting opinions from two of the Northern justices, went on to pronounce judgment on the Missouri Compromise. He declared that the Compromise was void, that slaves were property, and that Congress had no power to exclude them from a Territory. There was no need for him to have touched on the subject at all, but the gentle art of evading issues was not one of Taney's strong points. He thought he saw the Union and the Constitution endangered by the question of slavery in the Territories, and he was determined to write an opinion which would settle the question forever.

To the public it seemed that the Court had gone out of its way to perpetuate the inferior status of Negroes. Taney declared that "they had for more than a century before been regarded as beings of an inferior order . . . so far inferior that they had no rights which the white man was bound to respect; and that the Negro might justly and lawfully be reduced to slavery for his benefit."

Lincoln was appalled by the implications of the decision. If Congress could not prohibit slavery in a Territory, it followed that a Territorial legislature, created by Act of Congress, likewise had no power to do so. In other words, the decision marked the death knell of any attempt to get rid of slavery. The sacred right of property took precedence every time over the sacred right of freedom. The South was jubilant, not because Southerners, with the exception of a few fire-eaters, had ever dreamed seriously of extending slavery into the Territories, but because they were weary of the eternal wrangling over slavery and honestly believed that the Dred Scott decision had put an end to it.

The Republicans, far from bowing to a decision which would cut the ground from under their feet, reasserted their purpose of opposing the extension of slavery. Horace Greeley, hitherto an admirer of Taney, sneered at the decision as being no more entitled to respect than the idle chatter of a barroom. Seward, in the Senate, declared that the Republicans would override or reconstruct the Court. Most virulent of all were of course the abolitionists. Never had the Union with slaveholders seemed to them more obnoxious. Never had they echoed the cry of the fire-eaters—"the time for separation has come"—with more heartfelt conviction.

VII

The more Lincoln thought about the Dred Scott decision, the more convinced he was that it was the result of a conspiracy on the part of Douglas, Pierce, Taney and Buchanan, to foist slavery on the Territories. The idea preyed upon him, took possession of him, and finally swept him into the White House. We find it fully developed for the first time in a speech delivered at Springfield, Illinois, on June 16, 1858, before the Republican State Convention. The Convention had just made Lincoln its candidate for United States Senator. When he read the speech over to a few political cronies, they were startled by a sentence in the first paragraph. Lincoln had written that "a house divided against itself cannot stand," that the Nation could not endure half slave and half free. It was "a damned fool utterance," one friend told him, but Herndon exclaimed:

"Lincoln, deliver that speech as read and it will make you President." Lincoln said he had thought about it long enough, the time had come to say it: "If it is decreed that I should go down because of this speech, then let me go down linked to the truth."

The high point of Lincoln's speech that night was this very declaration: "A house divided against itself cannot stand. I believe this government cannot endure half slave and half free. I do not expect the house to fall but I do expect it will cease to be divided. It will become all one thing or all the other. Either the opponents of slavery will arrest the further spread of it, and place it where the public mind shall rest in the belief that it is in the course of ultimate extinction; or its advocates will push it forward till it shall become alike lawful in all the States, old as well as new, North as well as South."

Herndon was no doubt delighted that the "house divided" theme, which was hammered home in the debates with Douglas, laid Lincoln open to the charge of abolitionism. Hitherto he had been known as a moderate on the slavery question, and so he always thought of himself, but to Southerners he was forever afterward a Black Republican with a pronounced mania on the subject of slavery. By the time the Lincoln–Douglas debates were under way the fanatics had done their work so well that few people, North or South, could analyze the situation dispassionately. The Southern leaders chose to ignore Lincoln's further remarks about slavery, as did the abolitionists.

If they had followed the debates carefully, they would have seen that Lincoln expressly disclaimed any belief in the social and political equality of the two races. He repudiated the stigma of abolitionism and he insisted that he was as much in favor as any Southerner of keeping the white man on top. The South paid no attention. Lincoln was a Republican and therefore he must believe in the amalgamation of the two races. His almost mystical devotion to the Union was something that neither the fire-eaters nor the abolitionists ever understood. Whatever he did or failed to do about slavery was always inspired by that devotion. Military necessity eventually placed upon his shoulders the responsibility for emancipating the slaves, but if the war for the Union had gone as well as he hoped it would, slavery would not have been abolished by any act of his. As it was, the Emancipation Proclamation expressly omitted the loyal slave States from its terms. Slavery was an evil only if the slaveholder were in rebellion against the United States.

The abolitionists were not satisfied with the Emancipation Proclamation. From their point of view it was a sorry document, but they could afford to wait. On the day he made his "house divided" speech, Lincoln set forth on a long journey that could only end in their camp. Douglas, who was a better prophet than Lincoln, foresaw that the "house divided" doctrine led inevitably to "a war of sections, a war of the North against the South, of the Free States against the Slave States, a war of extermination to be continued relentlessly until the one or the other shall be subdued and all States shall become either free or slave." As long as Lincoln maintained that a nation cannot endure half slave and half free, that it was bound to become all one thing or all the other, he was heading in the same direction as the troublemakers. No matter how much he might insist that he had no intention of interfering with slavery where it existed already, or how loudly he proclaimed that he was not an abolitionist and that he was not a believer in racial equality, he had nonetheless worked himself into a position from which there was no escape except via peaceable secession or war.

In vain Douglas protested that the Dred Scott decision had changed nothing. It did not pave the way for the extension of slavery into the Free States or into the Territories. Slavery was utterly dependent on local support. With or without the decision, it would go where people wanted it, and not an inch further. Why had it failed to secure a foothold in Kansas? "Simply because," said Douglas, "there was a majority of her people opposed to slavery, and every slaveholder knew that if he took his slaves there, the moment the majority got possession of the ballot boxes, and a fair election was held, that moment slavery would be abolished and he would lose them." Why should the shrewd and virtuous Yankee deliberately adopt a system of labor that offended his sense of justice, and that he had proved to his own satisfaction was as inefficient as it was evil?

Douglas' arguments won him the Illinois election, but that was as far as he would ever go. He had alienated the Democratic politicians in the South by not positively approving of slavery, and he had alienated a substantial section of Northern opinion by not condemning it. Lincoln came out of the senatorial election with increased reputation. Any man who could hold his own with Douglas, and fire the zeal of the abolitionists without losing the support of the conservatives, had proved his qualifications for the highest office in the land.

It would be interesting to know how many of the Republicans who shouted themselves hoarse over Lincoln when they chose him as their standard bearer in 1860 had ever pondered over the implications of the "house divided" speech.

Those who had knew that Lincoln was not just a good stump speaker or a man who had not made any enemies, but a politician who had the ability to say "no." When Lincoln said "no" to the Crittenden proposals and to all other proposels of the kind, he certainly did not think of himself as slamming the door in the face of the peacemakers. It is true that when certain influential members of the Republican party were thought to be wavering, he wrote to his friend Lyman Trumbull urging him to stand firm, that "the tug of war has to come, and better now than at any time hereafter," but it does not follow from this one remark that he had resigned himself to the inevitability of civil war. On the contrary, he evidently expected the danger of war to evaporate under the fierce heat of Republican unity.

On his trip from Springfield to Washington in the winter of 1861, he assured the citizens of Buffalo that if they would only stand by their convictions and obligations, "the clouds now on the horizon will be dispelled." At Troy he declared that the country did not need to be saved, for "it will save itself," and in New York he told Frémont personally what he had told every audience he addressed, that he firmly believed peace would be preserved.

Lincoln said no to the compromisers because he feared that, unless the Republican party dug their toes in, the evils of slavery might well engulf the whole nation. Though slavery was already petering out in the Border States, though it had reached its limit of expansion in the Southwest, and though the civilized world was definitely moving away from it, Lincoln thought there was still enough life in it to destroy the great American experiment in self-government. A few Southerners in Congress conceded "that the demand they had so loudly made for admission of slavery to the Territories was really worth nothing to the institution of slavery." The whole fuss and storm, as James G. Blaine said, "related to an imaginary Negro in an impossible place." The invention of the threshing machine and the substitution of factory goods for the products of household industry all pointed to its gradual disappearance, yet to Lincoln and to many others the march of slavery seemed relentless and well planned.

Lincoln did not expect war, but he was willing to risk it in defense not merely of his own principles but of the cherished convictions of the Republican party. Admittedly the Republican party included a number of restless spirits, ex-Whigs and disgruntled Democrats, who could hardly be called idealists, but they were not the men Lincoln was bound to consider. The founders, the men who had borne the heat and burden of the day, had concentrated all their efforts on creating an antislavery party. Whether they were professed abolitionists or not, and many of them were, they had created the sentiment that Lincoln obeyed. Fortunately his own passion for the Union fitted in well with their refusal to consider any further compromise. The South had no grievances that they were aware of, and therefore all the talk of conciliation was irrelevant.

The American people might have liked to make one further effort to adjust their differences, but both the abolitionists and the fire-eaters saw to it that the democratic machinery broke down at the right time. The people were never consulted. In spite of monster petitions in favor of the Crittenden Compromise, they were never given a chance to vote on it. In the South, the ordinances of secession were rushed through in one State after another before the sober second thought of the inarticulate masses had a chance to express itself. Even so, it was no easy task to persuade the American people to fight each other. The German-born Carl Schurz told Lincoln early in 1861 that he must strike a vigorous blow at once if he wanted to rally the Free States to his administration, and in the Confederate capital friends of Jefferson Davis warned him that unless some decisive action were taken to establish its prestige, the Confederacy was in danger of crumbling to pieces.

The fanatics were desperate. Time was running out. If this opportunity slipped through their fingers, if another compromise were agreed upon, who knows—the South might have peered into the future and seen that slavery was doomed, that it would never live to see the twentieth century. Even if it were not swept away by the incalculable force of humanitarian sentiment, it would never be able to withstand the competition of the machine. Whenever a slave was made a mechanic, he was more than half freed. If the extinction of slavery through natural processes could have been foreseen, the abolitionist agitation would gradually have subsided, and along with it the demand for secession. Instead of excoriating slaveholders, abolitionists might have turned their minds to the underlying racial and social problems involved in emancipation, problems with which we are still struggling today.

But it was not to be. America would not wait. There are moments in the life of every nation when the people feel that the limit of human endurance has been reached. So it was a hundred years ago. Men told each other, some stridently and some philosophically, that the tug of war had to come, the sooner the better. They were weary of compromises. Put away the ballot boxes. Stop talking. Shout down the submissionists and the doughfaces. The time for action had come at last. For thirty years fanatics had been sowing dragons' teeth. Now they would reap the crop of iron men.

BIBLIOGRAPHICAL NOTES

These notes do not attempt to mention all the books and articles relevant to the subjects discussed in the preceding chapters. An invaluable introduction to the causes of the war is Thomas J. Pressly's *Americans Interpret Their Civil War* (1954). The object of these notes is merely to direct the reader to the more important sources from which the author has drawn the conclusions reached in this book.

ONE: *The Southern Fanatics*

The background of Southern conservatism is clearly presented in Russell Kirk's *Randolph of Roanoke: a Study in Conservative Thought* (1951). *The Conservative Mind* (1953) by the same author will also be found useful. Henry Adams' *John Randolph* (1898) is less favorable to Randolph.

The literature on Calhoun is voluminous. In addition to the three-volume biography by Charles M. Wiltse (1944-1951), now the standard work on the subject, August O. Spain's *The Political Theory of John C. Calhoun* may well be consulted. Spain gives a clear account of Calhoun's views on liberty and authority, the concurrent majority, the nature of the federal Union, and of his defense of slavery. Harriet

Martineau's *Retrospect of Western Travel* (London, 1838) shows us Calhoun, Clay and Webster, as they appeared to a shrewd and sympathetic traveler.

Laura A. White's *Robert Barnwell Rhett, Father of Secession* (1931) is invaluable for an understanding of South Carolina politics between the years 1830-1860, though as a portrait of Rhett it leaves something to be desired. *Frank Leslie's Illustrated Newspaper* (Feb. 9, 1861) contains one of the few contemporary descriptions of the celebrated fire-eater, and further glimpses of him will be found scattered through the fascinating pages of Mary Boykin Chesnut's *A Diary From Dixie* (1905). R. B. Rhett, Jr. contributed a eulogy of his father and a bitter arraignment of Jefferson Davis in the *Battles and Leaders of the Civil War* (1887), vol. I, *The Confederate Government in Montgomery*. The Charlestown *Mercury* which, as the organ of the Rhetts, reflects the views of the secessionists, should also be consulted.

The chief authority on Yancey is J. W. Du Bose, *The Life and Times of William Lowndes Yancey* (1892), a cumbersome, uncritical book, but it contains information not to be found elsewhere. Du Bose writes as a friend of Yancey's and his biography is full of reminiscences. It is particularly valuable when used in connection with Yancey's speeches. Many of these have been preserved in pamphlet form.

William G. Brown's *The Lower South in American History* (1902) includes a good essay on Yancey, showing the tremendous hold his oratory gave him over his generation. Henry Hilliard's description of Yancey in *Political Pen Pictures at Home and Abroad* (1893) is interesting as representing the point of view of a political opponent. Hilliard, who also came from Alabama, was a Southern Unionist. When Alabama seceded, he went with his State reluctantly. Further information about Yancey can be gleaned from Avery Craven's *The Coming of the Civil War* (1942), one of the indispensable books of the period. Craven is also the author of an excellent biography of Edmund Ruffin (1932), in which Ruffin's contributions to agriculture are traced along with his secessionist activities. Ruffin's diary has never been published. The fourteen folio volumes of manuscript covering the years 1856-1865 are in the Library of Congress.

How widely Southerners differed among themselves on the great issues of the day can be seen by consulting Dwight L. Dumond's *Southern Editorials on Secession* (1931). Further information on the development of the secession movement will be found in George Fort Milton's monumental biography of Stephen Douglas, *The Eve of Conflict* (1934) and in Clifford Dowdey's more popular *The Land They Fought For* (1955). Finally, no student of the period can afford to ignore Allan Nevins' great panorama of American history, *Ordeal of the Union* and *The Emergence of Lincoln* (1950). These titles (each two volumes) cover the period 1846-1861.

Two: *The Abolitionists*

The best general view of the abolition movement will be found in Albert Bushnell Hart's *Slavery and Abolition* (1906) and in Gilbert H. Barnes's *The Antislavery Impulse, 1830-1844* (1933). Hart, the son of an abolitionist, is inclined to attribute the success of the movement to the influence of William Lloyd Garrison. Barnes is critical of Garrison and of the New England Anti-Slavery Society, and gives more credit than Hart to James G. Birney, Theodore Dwight Weld and the more politically minded abolitionists.

By far the most important book about Garrison is the four-volume documentary *Life* written by his two sons, Francis Jackson and Wendell Phillips Garrison (1894). As his daughter says, the *Life* is "a quarry from which all subsequent lives have necessarily been written." The authors have allowed the documentary material to speak for itself. Students of the antislavery movement will want to consult the files of the *Liberator*, and they should also read John J. Chapman's eloquent tribute to the man he so passionately admired, *William Lloyd Garrison* (1913).

Wendell Phillips suffers from the lack of an adequate full-length biography, but *Two Friends of Man* by Ralph Korngold (1950) tells the story of Garrison and Phillips and their relationship with Lincoln. Richard Hofstadter's thoughtful essay on Wendell Phillips, the patrician as agitator, in *The American Political Tradition* (1948) should also be consulted.

James G. Birney and His Times (1890), by his son William Birney, attacks Garrison for urging his supporters not to vote or organize a political party against slavery. Benjamin P. Thomas, the author of the best one-volume biography of Lincoln in existence, has also written an admirable, short biography of Theodore Weld (1950).

A very different view of the antislavery movement will be found in Hilary A. Herbert's *The Abolition Crusade and its Consequences* (1912). Herbert, a Southerner who fought for the Confederacy, maintains that the vehemence of the Northern abolitionists effectually destroyed the movement for emancipation in the Southern States.

Oswald Garrison Villard's *John Brown 1800–1859: A Biog-*

raphy Fifty Years After (1910), is still the most thorough book on the subject, though Villard is inclined to idealize his hero. Robert Penn Warren's *John Brown, the Making of a Martyr* (1929) is less eulogistic.

The Memoir and Letters of Charles Sumner (1877-1893) is an old-fashioned biography, full of useful matter but uncritical. Laura A. White redresses the balance in her scholarly article on Sumner in *Essays in Honor of W. E. Dodd* (1935) proving that however much he hated slavery, Sumner was not as unalterably opposed to secession as he chose to appear once the war had started.

The hopelessness of colonization as a cure for the evils of slavery is trenchantly stated by Garrison in *Thoughts on African Colonization* (1832). To tip the scales, Launcelot M. Blackford shows in *Mine Eyes Have Seen the Glory* (1954) that colonization was a potent factor in breaking up the slave trade.

The growing rift between North and South on the subject of slavery can be traced in the twelve volumes of John Quincy Adams' *Memoirs*. Adams died in 1848. While too much of a politician to call himself an abolitionist, he served the anti-slavery cause well by championing the rights of free speech.

Henry Adams' *The Great Secession Winter of 1860-1861* (Mass. Hist. Soc. Procl., vol. 43) shows very clearly how close to compromise the Republican party came in January, 1861. Henry Adams was secretary to his father, Charles Francis Adams, at the time. The Adams family had no great respect for Lincoln and did not realize how actively he too was working against the forces of compromise.

The *Autobiography* of Charles Francis Adams, Jr. covers the same period.

THREE: *The Search for the Middle Way*

The earlier historians of the Civil War, such as John A. Logan (*The Great Conspiracy: Its Origin and History*), 1886, John W. Draper (*History of the American Civil War*), 1867-70, and Herman E. von Holst (*Constitutional and Political History of the United States*), 1877-92, pay little attention to the last-minute efforts at compromise. They depicted the war as a struggle between right and wrong. The victory of the North was the climax of a great moral drama. Any detailed discussion of the frantic efforts to avoid the war, efforts that so nearly succeeded, would merely blur the picture.

James Ford Rhodes is the first of the great historians to attempt a dispassionate study of the causes of the war. His opinions were grounded on the conviction that in history, as he phrased it, "all the right is never on one side and all the wrong on the other." The Rhodes family came from New England, and he himself grew up in Cleveland during the war. Like all good Northerners, he believed that "it was an unrighteous cause which the South defended by arms." It is all the more remarkable therefore that he should have written as he did about the Crittenden Compromise. He blames the Republicans for its defeat. He asserts that if it had passed, it would have prevented the secession of the Cotton States, other than South Carolina, "and the beginning of the Civil War in 1861." (J. F. Rhodes, *History of the United States, 1850-1877*, vol. III, 155.)

Allan Nevins agrees with Rhodes that in rejecting the Crittenden Compromise, "the Republicans had taken what history later proved to have been a fearful responsibility, just as in thrusting secession forward the Southern extremists were taking the same responsibility." (Allan Nevins, *The Emergence of Lincoln*, I, 398.)

J. G. Randall thinks that "intransigents on both sides, antislavery enthusiasts no less than ardent secessionists, opposed not only compromise 'terms' but the very idea of any compromise whatever."

David M. Potter in *Lincoln and His Party in the Secession Crisis* (1942) has examined the whole question of the possibility of compromise in great detail. He asks the questions that the earlier historians ignored. Could Lincoln have saved the Union without compromise? Could he have saved it without war? The answer would seem to be that if Lincoln had strengthened the hands of Southern Unionists by coming out strongly for compromise, he might have avoided the war and at the same time preserved the Union.

The arguments for and against this conclusion are discussed in Richard N. Current's *The Lincoln Nobody Knows* (1958). See particularly the fourth chapter, "The Man Who Said No."

Avery Craven, a Southerner of the "revisionist" school, goes further than Randall or Potter in criticizing Lincoln for fumbling and for his failure to adopt a clear-cut program. "He denounced the Dred Scott decision for declaring that a Negro could not be a citizen, yet declared that he himself was not in favor of Negro citizenship. He insisted on equal rights for all, yet bluntly disclaimed the doctrine of social equality for the races." (*The Coming of the Civil War*, 1957, p. 392.)

Charles W. Ramsdell goes still further than Craven in placing the responsibility for the Civil War, in the sense of the immediate outbreak of hostilities, squarely on the shoulders of Abraham Lincoln. ("Lincoln and Fort Sumter," in *The Journal of Southern History*, vol. III, p. 285.)

Less critical of Lincoln is Mary Scrugham's *The Peaceable Americans of 1860-1861: A Study in Public Opinion* (1921). In Miss Scrugham's opinion, four-fifths of the American people in 1860-61 favored compromise rather than civil war or dissolution of the Union. Without specifically blaming Lincoln, she feels that he did not reflect the will of the American people. Miss Scrugham's monograph is useful to any student of the period because of the extensive quotations from the correspondence of Republican politicians.

The question as to whether Lincoln made a mistake in opposing the compromisers instead of supporting them brings us back to the question of slavery. If there was a real danger of slavery extending into the Territories and overrunning the Free States, as Lincoln evidently feared, then unquestionably he was right in refusing to compromise and in accepting the possibility of war. If the natural limits of slavery expansion had already been reached, as Clay, Webster and Douglas believed, then surely Lincoln was mistaken in insisting that the tug of war had to come, "the sooner the better."

A great deal of evidence can be produced to support both these positions. The question has recently been examined in great detail by Harry V. Jaffa in his *Crisis of the House Divided* (1959). Jaffa thinks that slavery was still very much a going concern in 1860, and that Lincoln was right in fearing that it might eventually spread over the whole country. In support of his argument, he cites Kenneth M. Stamp's *The Peculiar Institution* (1956), an exhaustive study of the economic and social status of slavery in the antebellum South. Stamp maintains that the claim that slavery had "about reached its zenith in 1860" and was on the verge of collapse is far from convincing. At the end of his chapter on the profit and loss of slavery, Stamp also says: "The idea that free labor under any circumstances can be employed more cheaply than slave is patent nonsense."

L. C. Gray's *History of Agriculture* (1933) might also be cited in support of Lincoln's fear that geography, climate and time would never of themselves put an end to slavery: "The often expressed idea that the slavocracy was about to become moribund for lack of territory for expansion appears to have little foundation. The lower South in 1860 contained land enough to admit of an increase of slave population for many decades."

On the other side of the argument, special mention must be made of Charles W. Ramsdell's famous essay, "The Natural Limits of Slavery Expansion" in the *Mississippi Valley Historical Review*, vol. XVI (1929) and "The Changing Interpretation of the Civil War" in the *Journal of Southern History* (1937), from which so much of the revisionist interpretation stems.

Richard Hofstadter, a Northerner whose sympathies incline to abolitionism rather than to slaveholders, thinks that "historians are in general agreement with such contemporaries of Lincoln as Clay, Webster, Douglas and Hammond that the natural limits of slavery expansion had already been reached. But even if slavery had spread into new territories, it hardly follows that it would have spread into the free states of the North." (*The American Political Tradition*, 1948, p. 117.)

The same point of view is reflected in J. G. Randall's masterly volumes, *Lincoln the President* (1945) and *Lincoln the Liberal Statesman* (1947). Ulrich B. Phillips, though he is inclined to look back at the Old South through rose-colored spectacles, argues that slavery on the whole was unprofitable. (*American Negro Slavery*, 1918.)

Perhaps the strongest support for the theory that slavery was doomed can be found in a book that the Republicans used as a campaign document in 1860, Hinton R. Helper's *The Impending Crisis of the South*, published in 1857. Helper was a North Carolinian, the son of a poor blacksmith. He addressed himself to the millions of small farmers, artisans, shopkeepers and clerks of the South, who had no slaves themselves, but who had come to believe that their social status depended on the preservation of the existing system. There was no trace in his work of any sympathy for the Negro. Slavery, he contended, enriched a few white men and injured all the others, and if he could have had his way all the slaves would have been sent back to Africa. With an imposing array of statistics, he demonstrated the vast superiority of the Free States in trade, agriculture, industry and education. The rapid progress of the North and the West convinced Helper that the South was being tragically outdistanced. The idea of the Free States deliberately inflicting the economic curse of slavery upon themselves would have seemed to Helper utterly preposterous.

Index

INDEX

Adams, Charles Francis, 129, 151, 152, 166, 179
Adams, Charles Francis, Jr., 157
Adams, Henry, 20
Adams, John Quincy, 24, 25, 28, 66
Adams, Samuel, 27, 33, 112
Alcott, Bronson, 90
Alcott, Louisa, 144
Anderson, Major Robert, 152, 171, 176
Andrew, John A., 130
Austin, William, 112

Barnwell, Senator Robert W., 38
Beauregard, General Pierre G. T., 176
Beecher, Lyman, 101
Bell, John, 10, 65
Beman, Reverend Nathan, 40
Benton, Senator Thomas Hart, 48
Bigelow, John, 77
Bigler, Sen. William, 162
Birney, James G., 115-119, 131
Blaine, James G., 194
Blair, Frank P., Jr., 180
Blow, Captain Peter, 186

Breckinridge, John C., 64, 69, 149, 161
Brooks, Preston, 127, 128
Brown, John, 7, 11, 53, 54, 80, 120, 131-146, 149, 150, 182
Brown, Governor Joseph E., 76
Buchanan, President James, 158, 160, 168, 172, 181, 189
Burke, Edmund, 18
Butler, Senator Andrew P., 126

Calhoun, Senator John C., 15-17, 20-23, 25-30, 32-41, 44, 45, 85, 86, 116, 121
Cass, Senator Lewis, 126
Chaffee, Dr. Charles, 187
Chandler, Senator Zachariah, 80, 168, 169
Channing, Rev. W. Ellery, 100, 111
Chapman, John J., 104
Chesnut, Mrs. James (Mary Boykin), 53, 70
Chesnut, John, 9
Clay, Henry, 15, 17, 26, 36, 37, 38, 46, 95, 118, 123, 150, 159, 166, 178

Clingman, Thomas L., 44, 45
Cobb, Howell, 115
Collamer, Senator Jacob, 162
Crittenden, Senator John J., 11,
123, 159-161, 163, 165-167, 175,
180, 184, 193, 194

Davis, Jefferson, 9, 45, 48, 50, 64,
68, 72-75, 77-79, 86, 109, 151,
161, 163, 175, 195
Davis, Mrs. Jefferson, 151
Doolittle, Senator James R., 162
Douglas, Senator Stephen A., 10,
45, 48-52, 60-65, 149, 162, 166,
167, 180, 183, 189, 190, 191
Dow, Neal, 175

Elmore, Franklin, 116
Earle, Dr., 43
Emerson, Dr. John, 186, 187
Emerson, Ralph Waldo, 53, 137,
144

Faneuil, Peter, 112
Forbes, Hugh, 137
Franklin, Benjamin, 29
Fremont, John C., 182, 185, 193

Garibaldi, Giuseppe, 137
Garrison, William Lloyd, 7, 8, 11,
46, 80, 86-91, 93-94, 96-102, 104-
109, 111, 113-116, 118, 120, 124,
129, 131, 176, 177
Greeley, Horace, 53, 167, 189
Green, Israel, 142
Grimes, Senator James W., 162

Hamilton, Alexander, 29
Hancock, John, 112

Harrison, President William H.,
117
Hay, John, 154, 173
Henry, Patrick, 27, 33, 38
Herndon, William, 184, 185, 190
Howe, Samuel Gridley, 149
Hugo, Victor, 144
Hunter, R. M. T., 162

Jackson, Andrew, 26, 40, 41
Jackson, General T. H. (Stonewall), 145
Jefferson, Thomas, 19, 27, 94, 95,
96

Kosciusko, General Tadeusz A.,
106

Lafayette, Marquis de, 73, 141,
142
Lee, General Robert E., 29, 106
Lincoln, Abraham, 7, 10, 41, 42,
51, 62, 63, 65-70, 75, 76, 78, 105,
118, 129, 149, 151, 153-158, 162-
165, 167, 170-176, 178-195
Longfellow, Henry Wadsworth,
53
Lovejoy, Rev. Elijah P., 30, 111,
112, 120
Lowell, James Russell, 169, 170
Lundy, Benjamin, 91-94, 97
Lyman, Theodore, 107-109
Lyons, Lord, 153, 154

Madison, James, 16, 95
Magrath, Judge A. G., 70
Marshall, Chief Justice John, 95
Martineau, Harriet, 16, 17
Mason, George, 19

Mason, James Murray, 78
Monroe, James, 95

Nevins, Allan, 38
Nicolay, John G., 154

Otis, Harrison Gray, 100, 103, 107, 113

Paine, Thomas, 101
Parker, Judge Richard, 143
Parker, Theodore, 124
Perry, Benjamin, 42, 43
Petigru, James L., 24, 155
Phillips, Wendell, 7, 11, 80, 110-113, 120, 123, 124, 129, 131, 160, 176, 177, 184, 185
Pickens, Francis W., 75
Pierce, Franklin, 50, 67, 72, 181
Polk, President James K., 34, 35, 118
Porter, David, 174
Potter, David, 155
Powell, Senator L. Whitehead, 162
Pryor, Roger, 79
Pugh, Senator George E., 64, 158

Quincy, Josiah, 20

Randall, John G., 59
Randolph, John, 11, 17-21, 23, 30
Rhett, Robert Barnwell, 7, 8, 9, 11, 23-29, 31-36, 38, 39, 42, 49, 60, 62, 66, 69, 70, 71, 73, 74, 76-78, 85, 86, 181
Rhodes, James Ford, 161
Rice, Senator Henry M., 162
Rolfe, John, 18

Ruffin, Edmund, 7, 9, 55-58, 60, 63, 66, 79, 80, 145, 176
Rutledge, John, 27

Sanford, John F. A., 187
Schurz, Carl, 195
Scott, Dred, 186-187, 189, 192
Scott, General Winfield, 67
Sedgwick, General John, 126
Seward, William H., 9, 54, 60, 68, 150-155, 162-164, 169, 170, 171, 174
Slade, William, 31
Slidell, John, 64, 78
Smith, Gerrit, 149
Smith, Robert Barnwell, see Rhett, Robert Barnwell
Stephens, Alexander, 45, 61, 68, 172
Stone, George Washington, 44
Stowe, Harriet Beecher, 52, 53, 54, 127, 128
Stuart, J. E. B., 141, 142
Sumner, Senator Charles, 11, 31, 80, 120-128, 130, 177, 181, 184

Taney, Chief Justice Roger B., 187-189
Tappan, Arthur, 99
Tappan, Lewis, 119, 120
Thayer, Eli, 134
Thompson, George, 105, 106, 109, 110, 120
Thoreau, Henry D., 137
Tocqueville, Alexis de, 95
Todd, Francis, 98
Toombs, Senator Robert, 35, 70, 161, 163, 165
Toynbee, Arnold, 33

Trumbull, Lyman, 164, 193
Tucker, St. John, 19
Turner, Nat, 87, 106
Tyler, John, 168

Van Buren, President Martin, 28, 33
Vance, Zebulon, 76
Vesey, Denmark, 95
Villard, Henry, 158

Wade, Senator Ben, 162, 177, 181
Washington, Judge Bushrod, 95
Washington, President George, 27, 29
Washington, Colonel Lewis, 140
Webster, Daniel, 15-17, 37, 38, 123
Weed, Thurlow, 163-5

Weld, Theodore, 118, 119
Welles, Gideon, 173
Whitman, Walt, 15
Whitney, Eli, 29, 37
Whittier, John Greenleaf, 20, 37, 53, 99
Wigfall, Louis T., 31
Wilberforce, William, 105
Wilkes, Captain Charles, 78
Wilmot, David, 34
Wise, Governor Henry A., 145, 146, 149

Yancey, William Lowndes, 7, 9, 11, 39-47, 49, 51, 52, 56-58, 60-66, 68, 71-75, 78, 79, 158, 160
Yeamans, Sir John, 24